All You Need
To Know About

Music
& The
Internet
Revolution

Conrad Mewton
Foreword by Alan McGee

about the author

Conrad Mewton is a music lawyer with the leading UK entertainment/media law practice at Denton Wilde Sapte. He previously worked as a "talent" lawyer at Spraggon, Stennett, Brabyn, whose clients include Prodigy, Ash, Gomez, Sugababes and Asian Dub Foundation. Prior to his time as a music lawyer, he was bass player in the rock band Mainstream, signed to Nude Records in the UK and Sony Entertainment worldwide. He was educated at Exeter University; St John's College, Oxford; and the College of Law, York.

All You Need
To Know About

Music
& The
Interne
Revolution

6/02

.333

Printed in the United Kingdom by Biddles Ltd, Surrey

Published by Sanctuary Publishing Limited, Sanctuary House,
45-53 Sinclair Road, London W14 0NS, United Kingdom

www.sanctuarypublishing.com

ISBN: 1-86074-325-0

acknowledgements

The author would like to thank Paul Spraggon, Sarah Stennett and Andrew Brabyn for their help in bringing about the successful completion of this book.

contents

foreword

by Alan McGee

The music industry is changing. I left Creation not to restart an old Creation idea but to start a company that Creation would have wanted to be, if it had begun in 2000. I don't think that record companies in their present form are really relevant any more. I think the future lies in multimedia film, radio, club, editorial content and music, and the Digital Age will be the key to this. The Poptones web site will sell CDs and offer downloads (both free and for a fee), show our films, broadcast our radio programmes, webcast our gigs and display opinions from our artists on everything from music to politics. For me, it *has* to be an all-encompassing experience. I couldn't do that with Creation and Sony, so I started Poptones. Our web site will hopefully grow one day to be a living, breathing beast that exists in its own world.

The advancement of the Digital Age gives us back the means of distribution of media, whether this is music or film. For me, these are the most exciting times. I believe that we're heading towards a subscription-based model (and I have done for three years – check the interviews). If you're going to buy a CD, it has to be price sensitive – £9.99 – look great, have great packaging and sound great. All pretty obvious stuff, except if you're the BPI – £14.99 for the CD and something that feels like data when you handle it. The internet revolution has only just begun. The technology is already in place. We just need broadband to actually happen and local calls to be free, and then the world will truly change. Enjoy this book.

Alan McGee is MD of the Poptones record label and, as former boss of the Creation label, the man responsible for signing Primal Scream and Oasis.

introduction

I t might seem a little odd for me to begin this book about the internet's seismic impact on the music industry by casting my mind back to the music revolutions of the '70s and '80s, but as I was downloading a track from Primal Scream's excellent *Xtrmntr* album from Napster the other day (purely for research purposes, you understand) a thought occurred to me.

There seemed something a little subversive, dangerous even, about what I was doing. I knew that this was not how Sony had intended me to listen to the album, and I guess I realised that there was no chance of either the band or their label being paid. (Actually, I did go out and buy the album afterwards on the strength of what I'd heard on my tinny little computer speakers.) Still, it struck me that something very revolutionary was happening to the way in which I and other music fans like me were now listening to music.

I also have a few mates who make their own dance stuff in their bedrooms, using little more than a battered old Atari and Steinberg's Cubase music software program – bootlegged, of course! They're always downloading samples and loops posted by other DIY music enthusiasts on the internet. So, I figured, the net isn't just affecting the way in which people listen to music but also how they *make* music, and that hasn't happened since, well, the Chicago house scene of the late '80s, or the suburban punk movement of the '70s.

the new punk...

The punk rock movement or 1976-78 had a significant impact on the music industry. *NME* journalists have a tendency to wax lyrical about the days of Johnny Rotten, Joe Strummer *et al*, although any musical trend that allowed the likes of Sham 69 and Billy Idol to flourish can't have been all good! It did, however, make it possible for kids with little or no experience of playing music to believe that it was possible to form a band, get up on stage and just play. It shook up an industry that was dominated by an indulgent, affluent rock scene, and what had previously been viewed as a closed shop was suddenly overrun by the disaffected, disenfranchised youth of English suburbia. Well, Paul Weller, anyway.

Records were made cheaply, recorded live and raw with little fuss. Small independents – Stiff, 2-Tone, Radar, Beggars Banquet, Factory and Rough Trade, among others – sprang up in punk's wake. Punk and new wave was a thriving musical scene, although as much of its importance was in setting fashion trends and creating a street culture filtered through a white, middle-class art-school perspective.

Punk has definite parallels with today's internet revolution of the music industry: the triumph of the do-it-yourself independent spirit of musicians taking the creation and distribution of music into their own hands; the development of an underground sub-culture (MP3, ripping, burning CDs, illegally trading music, setting up and running web sites as forums for the exchange of music fans' opinions, starting internet record labels); a belief held by kids that the music industry's traditional way of doing things is there to be overturned.

What the internet revolution lacks so far is a coherent musical direction. In fact, it's not really very much about the music, rather more a way of getting music heard without using a record label, listening to it without paying for it. It's also, unlike punk, a technology-based revolution. Without digital technology – modems, cables, PCs, encoders, decoders and the rest – it wouldn't be happening. With punk, a few safety pins and a couple of barre chords and you were away.

...or the new house?

In many ways, the MP3/internet revolution has as much in common with the Chicago house scene of 1986 and 1987. House music had its origins in new technology: digital recording equipment and, in particular, samplers. Kids in their bedrooms created their own sounds, collaging and mixing in other people's records over programmed drum beats, so house music – in its primitive form – was born. At the same time, vinyl culture was kept alive by the twin turntables and white-label 12" mixes of Chicago house DJs. Step forward ten years and internet technology is bringing access to the music industry to a new (repetitive beat) generation of DJs, dance labels, cut-and-paste post-modernists and, er, indie boys and their guitars.

Valid as either of these comparisons may be, the internet revolution has the potential to be more far-reaching than punk or house in instigating change within the music industry – in the way that records are distributed and marketed, in the way that rights are divided and retained by musicians and music is bought and listened to, and in the way that outside players – ISPs and telecommunications companies, for example – will gain a foothold in the music industry. Whether it will help spawn a vital new musical movement, as vital as punk or house, is another matter altogether. God knows the industry needs one.

the positive impact of the internet

The electronic delivery of music over the internet has the potential to be one of the best things ever to happen to the music industry. The threat of uncontrollable copyright theft may be giving labels and artists alike a collective morale deficit the size of the Guatemalan national debt, but the tone of this book is unashamedly positive, because there's a lot to be positive about. Here are just a few of the exciting ways in which the internet is influencing for the better the way that we create, exploit and listen to music. (All of these points are covered in greater depth later in the book.)

...On Record Labels And Publishers

Record labels now have the ability to target and reach niche audiences. Online marketing can promote releases far and wide in territories which labels could normally never afford to spend money breaking. Old catalogue can be reissued and repackaged (again). Labels can sell direct to the fans without always having recourse to traditional retailers and, of course, without having to deduct the retailer's margin from their profits. Fans can be forewarned of new releases and tours. With improvements in technology, particularly broadband and faster internet access, downloading music will become increasingly popular, leading to a corresponding decline in the cost of housing and shipping huge boxes of CDs. Eventually, these costs could even be eliminated altogether, which should mean much higher profit margins for record companies, giving them the opportunity to charge consumers less and to pay artists more. (Of course they will!)

...On Musicians

Internet music providers such as Peoplesound, Musicmaker, Musicunsigned and a host of others are offering exciting new opportunities to bands and their fans. Unsigned musicians can promote themselves to record companies and publishers via these promotional web sites. For named artists who have already established a loyal and core following through selling records by the traditional methods, the internet represents a fantastic opportunity for reaching that fanbase without the need for a record company to act as a go-between. The revolution in recording and distributing music brought about by the internet gives musicians the opportunity to create and sell their own music directly to their fans.

...On You, The Music Fan

Talk about consumer power! The internet is all about choice, choice and more choice. Music fans have never had it so good. Okay, all of the members of Boyzone are threatening to make solo records, but all the more reason to search the net far and wide for obscure back catalogue that even HMV hasn't room to stock. Or, if you've exhausted The Small Faces' *oeuvre* and you want to come right up to date, you can follow the progress of your favourite band's new album – *à la* Radiohead, Beck, Stereophonics – or discover what Axl Rose has been eating for breakfast during his ten years as LA's most famous recluse. Gigs, too, are open to all on the web. Fans too young or distant to attend can watch live webcasts streamed directly into their homes.

The net caters for every variety of musical style, so you can gain access to outtakes and net-exclusive free downloads from Supergrass, catch up with the latest cutting-edge dance movement at Ministryofsound.com or check out Jimmy Page jamming with The Black Crowes in some Midwestern amphitheatre. Send in your reviews of albums, go online for a live chat with Richard Ashcroft or spend years deciphering the lyrics to every song written by the Canterbury scene bands and post the results on the web. (Actually, someone already has. I've seen it, all 22 minutes of Caravan's 'Nine Feet Underground', Matching Mole, Robert Wyatt's 'The End Of An Ear' – they're all there.) Even if your sole reason for going online is to pay homage at the shrine of the This Is Spinal Tap web site, your life will have been enriched in some small way.

the online revolution

The full impact of the internet is still some way short of being fully realised and understood. However, it is already bringing significant changes to the way we view the music industry, the way we listen to music and the way we feel about the retail experience and shopping for records. It may even end up altering the way we view music itself – for example, should music be free for anyone to listen to whenever they want, in any form they want? And all of these changes bring with them legal and business complications – new laws, new contractual issues, new business models.

With all of the doubts, fears and general confusion surrounding the online revolution's impact on the record industry, it's easy to lose sight of the fact that the internet is a music-friendly technology, there to be embraced and utilised to suit the ends of artists, labels and fans alike. As this book demonstrates, music and the internet are ideally and uniquely suited to one another. There are plenty of problem areas to overcome, not least in combating MP3 piracy and in establishing a coherent structure and culture of paying for music online, but there are also some fantastic internet-created opportunities waiting to be grasped by the key players in the music industry. And for the rest of us, a whole new exciting world of discovering and listening to music is opening up before us.

music on the internet

the internet age

You knew that the music business had well and truly entered the Internet Age when the promotional campaign for Radiohead's *Kid A* album centred almost exclusively on the net. Eschewing conventional promo tools, such as videos or singles, the band (champions of MP3 and the promotional powers of the net) instead put out a series of ten- to 40-second "video blips" on the internet to accompany the release of the album, which were e-mailed as promotional tools direct to fans and media. The success of the campaign was no surprise – after all, fans had been weaned on a diet of *Kid A* outtakes, gossip and diaries from the inner sanctum of the recording studio throughout the making of the album, all posted not in snippets in the weekly music press, as in the past, but electronically, via the band's web site.

From Thom Yorke to Mick Hucknall and from Chuck D to Courtney Love, rock stars across the globe are now preaching the new gospel of the worldwide web. So before we go any further, we can safely dispense with the old cultural stereotypes about the internet being the domain of geeks, nerds and, er, military scientists. Welcome to cyberspace, the nerve centre of the new music revolution.

To keep up with the new order, you're going to need a basic understanding of the internet. For musicians and the music industry, this is a prerequisite for the successful exploitation (and negotiating the exploitation) of music online. It's also pretty essential for music fans whose interest in the internet extends no further than knowing the best way to obtain a copy of Half Man Half Biscuit's seminal 7" 'Dickie Davies Eyes'. This chapter will be mercifully brief, as most of us have a fairly good idea what the internet is; but for those of you who have been otherwise engaged line-dancing in the Outer Hebrides (or working in the music industry), here's a quick look at what you've missed…

so, what is the internet?

Most of us have a picture of the internet as an enormous link-up of the world's computers. In fact, although this is a pretty accurate image, it would be more correct to describe the internet as a global network of hardware and software which stores and transports information from a content provider to an end user. This infrastructure allows anyone who wants to say anything to say it to the world.

Information on the internet is stored on a whole suite of machines maintained by internet service providers, individuals and corporations. This information is linked via the world's telephone, satellite and radio networks and is visible on home computers, new-generation mobile phones and other "internet-ready" devices.

how to get online

Getting connected to the internet is easier than ever. Once you've signed up to an internet service provider (ISP) and installed a modem (a device which converts computer data into an audio signal so that it can be sent down your phone line), you're ready to go. In fact, nowadays you don't even have to go to the trouble of buying a modem, as it will be pre-installed in your computer.

internet service providers

When you log onto the internet from your computer, you're activating a command which instructs the modem plugged into your phone socket to dial up the phone number of your local ISP.

ISPs are your gateways to the net. Among the best known are AOL (America OnLine), AltaVista, Demon, CompuServe and Netcom. Many ISPs now provide access to the net for free (*unmetered access*) or for an annual or monthly subscription. Increasingly, subscription charges are dropping, and soon access will be free for users while ISPs will make money from advertising and other e-commerce revenue streams. Anyone who can afford a basic PC, laptop or even a new-generation mobile phone will be able to access the net.

Signing up to an ISP grants you access to the various different components of the internet, the most significant of which are the worldwide web, e-mail and newsgroups.

how does information travel?

ISPs employ huge computers known as *servers* to connect you to those components that you'll need – the web server, the e-mail server and so on. Servers send data in digital form to and from its chosen destination using *protocols*, such as TCP/IP (Transmission Control Protocol/Internet Protocol), a universal syntax understood by different computers on different continents.

When you send an e-mail with a file attached, TCP/IP splits up the information into discrete bits, or *packets*, and sends it to your chosen destination by the most efficient route, via routers. This will often mean passing through a neighbouring continent or two!

using the web browser

Once connected to the internet, you'll need to use a program known as a web browser to access information. This will enable your computer to talk to hundreds of others around the world. The browser opens web sites and allows you to view web pages. (You can open several web pages simultaneously and move backwards and forwards between them.) Web browsers use the standard protocols described above to send and receive information.

how to find music web sites

using search engines

One of the most important components in the whole internet process is something called a *search engine*. A search engine is run from a web site by a company dedicated to providing the service of looking things up for you. They are a kind of massive yellow pages but with an international directory at their disposal that lists web sites from all around the world. In fact, search-engine companies have now developed into portals providing not only internet search facilities but also a whole range of different services, such as chat rooms and providing news updates and entertainment information.

When you double-click on the browser icon on your computer to access the internet, you'll arrive at a default setting, which is usually the address of a search engine. (Originally, my Mac automatically defaulted to the Excite search engine.) You won't need to use a search engine if you already know the exact URL (Uniform Resource Locator, otherwise known as the *domain name* or address) that you're looking for, in which case simply enter this in the appropriate box at the top of the screen. The URL will always be prefixed by www (worldwide web), and will usually be suffixed by .com or .co.uk – for example, http://www.thecharlatans.com. The .com suffix signifies an international URL, and is therefore more prestigious than the "mere" .co.uk tag.

You'll need to use a search engine if you don't know the exact URL. When you ask a search engine – such as Excite, AltaVista or Yahoo – to look up a web site for you (for example, if you type in the words "Red Hot Chili Peppers" and press Search), it runs a program on its own server with your query criteria as a parameter. You'll then be told that it has found, say, 127 sites with references to Red Hot Chili Peppers, some of which will possibly be culinary references, but you can ignore these!

You can now visit your favourite band's web sites in the USA, Germany, Sweden or wherever one has been started up. Most will be unofficial and run by fans eager to exchange news and stories with others, but the band (or its record company – more on this later) will also host an official web site, where you can take part in competitions (win Flea's boxer shorts from the '95 tour, for instance!), buy concert tickets and merchandise, etc.

playing music on the internet

what do you need?

Okay, we're now nearly ready for the exciting bit: music on the net. Let's quickly recap by running through the "net essentials". To access music on the internet, you will need:

- An internet-enabled device of some sort, probably a PC or a Mac. (Internet access is easier on an iMac, which is designed to make getting online as simple as possible. It comes with everything you need to connect to the net – modem, web browser, ISP software – already pre-installed.) Internet access can also be obtained through WAP-enabled and third-generation mobile phones, television set-top boxes and even digital watches! (Check out Casio's MP3 watch at http://www.casio.com);

- To hook up with an ISP. There are hundreds to choose from and several factors to consider. The main one is price – as mentioned earlier, many are now free to sign up to (although they may well charge you for technical support, and at a prohibitive rate) while others charge a monthly fee but provide free technical assistance. With either option, until unmetered access becomes the norm you'll still be charged for phone calls, so sign up to an ISP charging only local rates. There are also other issues to consider, in particular the number of e-mail addresses and amount of free web space you'll be allocated. (We'll look at these more closely in Chapter 7.) At the time of writing, AOL, Virgin, BT Internet, AltaVista, Demon and Freeserve are the most popular ISPs. There are also some music-oriented ISPs, such as Madasafish or, of course, David "internet-addict" Bowie's very own Bowienet service at http://www.davidbowie.com;

- Access to a search engine or similar device to search for your favourite band's web site. Appendix II contains a list of the main music portals and web sites, including unsigned music sites, record company sites and so on;

- A virtual music player. This will differ depending on whether you're using a Mac or PC and on the music file format you're using, but nearly all virtual music software is downloadable for free. Appendix I lists a run-down of the best MP3 players currently available;

- PC speakers. Again, the best of these are listed in Appendix I. Alternatively, you could forsake PC speakers altogether and purchase a phono cable to run from your computer's audio output socket to your hi-fi, or play your MP3s on your new portable player…

- A portable MP3 player, allowing you to listen away from those dreaded PC speakers. The market leaders are Multimedia's Diamond Rio 500 (available for around £120 from http://www.riohome.com) and the Soundmaster (£80 from http://www.absolutemm.com).

the MP3 revolution

ch-ch-ch-changes

How many of the following buzzwords do you recognise? MP3, webcast, stream, RealAudio, digital download, WAP, e-commerce, "third-generation" mobile phone, ADSL, SDMI, CIA. Okay, the Central Intelligence Agency's links with the music industry have never been proven, but what about the others? If you'd bought a book on the music industry, say, five years ago, the chances were you wouldn't have come across any of those names. It's incredible how far the industry has evolved in such a short space of time.

There's a lot of hype about the internet in the media, and everyone's sick of hearing about the latest overnight "dotcom" millionaire (invariably some public-school drop-out with mates in the City); but the internet really has had a huge impact on the way people listen to music. In consequence, the record industry is in turmoil as it struggles to come to terms with artists' new-found freedom, the consumer's power to buy music from anywhere in the world for the cheapest price, the fear of a music-for-free MP3 subculture and the threat of service providers and telecommunications companies muscling in on its territory.

At the same time, the industry is excited about the potential to generate billions of pounds' worth of new revenues via the internet, including "pay-per-listen" subscription web sites, licensing to internet radio stations, expanding into new markets, selling back catalogue the world over, marketing and developing artists in new territories, downloading and streaming revenues, lucrative webcast concert link-ups, even billion-dollar mergers with ISPs. The possibilities are endless.

In this and the next couple of chapters, we'll take a look at all of those buzzwords and examine what they mean for the music industry, for the internet-empowered musician and for the way in which the rest of the planet will listen to its music.

how is music delivered on the internet?

physical delivery

Although the music industry is spending most of its time coming to terms with music being downloaded or digitally distributed, music can of course be physically delivered to your house as a result of ordering it via the internet – in other words, you treat the internet as a record store, browse through all of the CDs available and click on the ones you wish to purchase. You then type in your credit card details on a form which only the shop you're buying from can see and a few days later the CD arrives in the post.

Whether a new technology has the capacity to really grip the public's imagination and become a success will often come down to one simple but brilliant idea or chance occurrence – in this case, the size and shape of a CD. When you think about it, the music industry is ideally placed to capitalise on the 21st-century home-shopping boom. The covers of CDs are easily reproducible on screen; you can hear extracts from the album (audio clips) before deciding whether to buy; and CDs, like paperbacks (although very little else), are the perfect shape for pushing through your letterbox. For this reason alone, sales of CDs over the net will snowball, even if the hot air carrying the rest of the home-shopping boom evaporates.

E-commerce sales (as sales of physical records over the internet are referred to) have soared over the past twelve months or so. These now account for around 3% of the total market for music. (In 1999, e-commerce sales had a market share of just 0.3%.) At the moment, sales of physical product over the internet far outweigh the number of tracks being (legitimately) digitally downloaded, but this could all be about to change…

digital delivery

The internet has brought about a revolution in the way music is distributed. Before now, the only way of doing things was to record the artist's performance to tape and then transfer that performance to disk, to be distributed and sold in the form of CDs, cassettes and vinyl. The advent of the internet makes the digital delivery of those performances a reality.

The premise of digital delivery is extraordinary yet entirely logical: the aim is to transfer all of the digital information contained on a normal physical CD without also transferring the bit of plastic containing that information. Music becomes binary code, a series of 0s and 1s, joining the worldwide flow of digital information. You can see how frighteningly unstoppable it all suddenly seems, particularly to the people who own the rights in those 0s and 1s and want payment for their use. (We'll look at this later.)

To travel across the cables of the internet, the music must first be converted into a digital audio file that can be stored on a hard drive and then played through your computer. Because high-fidelity music involves large amounts of digital information (a typical CD holds up to 700 megabytes of data), transferring music over the internet is a slow business for most of us. At the time of writing, it can still take anywhere from ten minutes to half an hour to download one five-minute song, depending on the capacity of your modem (so don't try downloading 'Free Bird' just yet).

what is broadband internet?

The future looks more promising for the digital delivery of music as we move towards what is known as *broadband internet*. This is where things start to get a bit technical, I'm afraid, but the upshot of these new developments will mean faster access to the internet and therefore music fans will be able to download songs in real time with near-perfect CD audio quality. Soon it will take seconds rather than minutes to download a song. In other words, you will be able to download music faster than it actually takes to play it.

Currently, most users access the internet via modems carrying between 14.4 and 56.6 kilobits of data per second. With two new broadband technologies soon to reach the market, access will be up to 30 times faster: cable internet will access the internet via current cable TV lines and special modems, while BT's ADSL (Asymmetric Digital Subscriber Line) will be capable of receiving and sending digital information at speeds of up to two megabits per second across existing telephone lines. Users will be able to subscribe to the ADSL service through their ISP.

With modems getting faster, unmetered access enabling more and more people to hook up to the net and compression technologies (which allow you to squeeze more audio data down the cables and telephone lines in one go) becoming increasingly sophisticated, the market share for digital music is sure to rise from its current, almost non-existent level.

the format for delivery

So far, we've looked in general terms at how music is downloaded by sending digital audio files across the wires from one computer to another. The vehicle in which these files travel (ie the way in which they're compressed to make their journey to your hard drive) is for you to choose. There is no one definitive format for sending digital information, and because the technology is still in a state of flux, at the moment most consumers are likely to choose the market leader – particularly if the market leader enables them to (legally or illegally) download their favourite songs for free!

As you can imagine, this is a controversial and sensitive subject for the record industry as it attempts to embrace the Internet Age. The industry is desperately hoping that a secure format – such as AT&T's a2b, Liquid Audio, IBM's Madison project or Microsoft's Windows Media Audio (WMA) – will become the standard for the delivery of downloadable music. All of these are software packages that utilise encryption technology (covered in detail in Chapter 11) and therefore, in theory, prevent the pirating of music.

However, representing the potential dark force of (whisper it) piracy is a currently unencrypted format known to its friends as MP3. MP3 is the format you've probably already heard of. In fact, like several other well-known brands, it's fast becoming synonymous with the delivery of music itself and, as it's the unquestioned market leader in digital downloads, it's also the most significant.

MP3 music

what is MP3?

In techno-speak, MP3 stands for Motion Picture Experts Group One, Audio Layer Three – a reference to its origins as an inter-standard compression program when it was invented in 1991 by a German research firm, initially for broadcast use. Of more interest to the world's music fans, the MP3 compression program operates as an open file format, allowing users to convert the masses of data that make up audio files into much smaller, near-CD-quality MP3 files.

how does MP3 work?

MP3 works by compressing packages of digital information – such as computer programs, video clips and songs – to approximately one twelfth of the size of a normal audio CD file (in the case of songs) while losing only negligible audio-quality fidelity. The files are decompressed on arrival at the end user's computer and can be played back on an MP3 player, which can be downloaded for free from web sites such as http://www.mp3.com.

music on the move

One of the biggest myths about MP3 is that, because it is a digital music format, it sounds exactly the same as any other digital format, such as CD. Not quite – at least, not until high-speed broadband access becomes a reality for most of us! For now, the problem is the extent to which MP3 files have to be compressed in order to make their journey to our hard drives.

Compression works by sifting through and deleting selected sound frequencies in order to enable the transmission of only the key frequency elements present in the music. The loss in sound frequencies affects the way your body responds to the music – you may not hear an obvious difference, but you'll probably feel one. The compression used in MP3s is so intense that a lot of the top end is usually lost and the bass is unnaturally emphasised. It's for this reason that MP3 is probably unsuitable for serious listening on hi-fi speakers at home.

For the time being, it seems more likely that MP3 will become the format of choice for music on the move. The format has several advantages over its main rivals in this area – MiniDiscs, CDs and cassettes – for the following reasons:

- MP3 players are tiny and have no moving parts, so they can't be jolted or disturbed during playback;

- They consume very little power, so a battery lasts for many hours of playback;

- They can store 32MB of data, with power to add (using SmartMedia cards, or a Memory Stick, in the case of the new Sony MP3 player);

- Using the Playlist functions (see Appendix II), you can program in a different selection of music to listen to each time you take your portable MP3 player out with you.

In the next two or three years, as the price of MP3 players looks set to drop and increased bandwidth and therefore higher transmission rates will mean an improvement in the overall sound of MP3 files, the Rio and its friends will offer a greater threat to traditional home hi-fis. In the meantime, however, portable is beautiful.

why all the fuss?

As MP3 is an international standard, being Windows friendly, Mac friendly and capable of being read by the countless software players flooding the market, it has gained support from all quarters, making it the format of choice for music fans. However, it poses a very real threat to the way in which the record industry does business.

Since MP3 is known as an *open architecture* format, not only is it an ideal way to send music files back and forth across the internet but, once it's downloaded, the information is freely copyable. One person can upload a song that they've downloaded from an MP3 file and can then make it available to millions. The repercussions of this are obviously huge, and we'll cover them later in the book.

do believe the hype!

One of the most quoted statistics in newspaper and web articles concerning the phenomenal rise of digitally deliverable music is that "MP3" is the second most popular search engine term requested after "sex". I don't know what this says about internet users, but maybe these people should get out more! Still, the more serious research makes for revealing reading. Stock-market analysts Sanford C Bernstein predict that the impact of the internet will mean that the recording industry will be receiving extra profits of $180 million a year by 2003, rising to as much as $500 million if an encrypted format for delivering downloads emerges as the industry standard instead of those sexy MP3s. Forrester Research, meanwhile, estimates that digital downloading alone will earn $1.1 billion for the US music industry by 2003.

At the opposite end of the spectrum, the online market research firm Jupiter Communications predicts that, in five years' time, the market for digitally downloaded music will be only about $30 million, a figure it describes as "anaemic" and which would represent only a tiny percentage of the $12 billion recorded market.

These figures show that there is still a lot of confusion and uncertainty surrounding the exact impact that the internet – and MP3 in particular – will have on the music industry. The reality, though, is that millions of people wired into the worldwide web have already discovered the MP3 format, and inevitably this will change the way in which the music industry operates. MP3 has already been endorsed by famous artists like David Bowie, Jimmy Page, Hole, Public Enemy and The Beastie Boys, all of whom have chosen the internet as the medium through which to distribute their music.

what are the alternatives to MP3?

The drive towards a viable alternative to MP3 has so far been spearheaded by a group known as SDMI, or the Secure Digital Music Initiative to give it its full title. SDMI is a forum in which music and technology companies swap views and ideas and undertake research with the common aim of developing an infrastructure that will enable the secure delivery of music content via a variety of delivery mechanisms over the internet. Broadly speaking, "secure delivery" means that the files will either be watermarked (like bank notes) or encrypted (ie scrambled into a code that only the end user is able to decode, on payment).

Over the past couple of years, several major information technology companies have worked hand in hand with the music industry to achieve this goal. The current forerunners in the race to achieve a market-standard platform for downloading (and to knock MP3 off its perch) are Microsoft's Windows Media Audio, Liquid Audio and AT&T's a2b. As well as providing high-quality audio performance, these software packages feature "rights management capabilities", with the idea of protecting encoded content for the owner's copyright. The plan is that downloading will be accomplished in encrypted format as a secure credit-card transaction. As yet, however, no one *de facto* standard has emerged to rival MP3, and with the nascent internet music culture still dominated by the MP3 file-sharing ethos of Napster, Freenet, Gnutella *et al*, there is no likelihood in the foreseeable future of MP3's pre-eminence being challenged.

how will we listen to music in the future?

music for free

No one thinks twice about turning on the television and settling down to watch the latest episode of *Frasier* or *Friends*. Both of these programmes are on commercial television (ie not funded by your licence fee), so you don't expect to pay to watch them. You know that ITV and Channel 4 earn billions of pounds from advertising revenue each year. You don't lie awake at night worrying that Jennifer Aniston will starve just because you didn't fork out a tenner to see her latest show. After all, TV people do all right, don't they?

We all expect to see our favourite TV programmes for free, because we've all grown up in a culture in which TV has always been readily available at the touch of a button. You don't go to it; it comes to you. There's now a very real possibility that the music industry is heading in exactly the same way. And the thing that's driving us towards a free-music-on-demand culture? You guessed it: the internet.

The internet makes music available at the click of a mouse. The MP3 file format allows the listener to download music for free, and the time is fast arriving where fans will be able to download their favourite artists' songs in seconds – and they won't expect to pay for the privilege. It may be hard for us to envisage, but already a new generation of young American college kids (all of whom have grown up with computers at home) think nothing of downloading a song from Freenet, Napster or Gnutella and e-mailing it to their mates. If you tried telling them that they were infringing copyright they'd look at you as if you were crazy, just as other people might be surprised if they were accused of infringing the actors' performing rights in *Friends*.

Commercial television, however, is based on an economic model that makes it viable to view programmes for free. The commercial TV industry makes its money through advertising. Advertisers, in turn, rely on ratings and marketing demographics to target their products at the right audiences. The music industry is still a very long way off developing a business model based on anything even remotely similar to TV broadcasting. The internet may well change all that, however, and, from a commercial perspective, it wouldn't be a bad thing if it did.

Just think of the way in which the television and motion-picture industry has developed a clever line in expanding the shelf life of its product. Take a new blockbuster movie – the latest James Bond, say. A new Bond movie is like a major album release by a superstar artist – a Madonna or a U2. You know roughly what you're going to get, you know that the production values will be state of the art and you can guarantee that the advertising spend would be enough to bankrupt Al Fayed several times over. But how much money will the record and film production companies recoup? How can they maximise income from the paying customer?

Let's look at the album release first. Madonna's *Music* is simultaneously released around the world and her fanbase rush out to buy it in its first week in the shops. Thereafter, sales gradually fall away, buoyed up by the occasional single release or tour. Six months or so after appearing, sales have slowed to a trickle and the record is, to all intents and purposes, dead. Now, let's compare that to the movie release.

Bond premières in the States and then goes nationwide to all major cinema chains. A good two months later, the movie hits Europe and plays to more packed houses. After four or five months, the movie is only being shown in selected cinemas, or has been relegated to smaller screens. No matter – a few months later, the video/DVD release hits retail and a second wave of income is generated. When sales from the video/DVD release have tailed off, the movie is then released to video rental libraries and a third, steadier stream of income is generated. Finally, the film is syndicated to Sky Box Office/Sky Movies/BBC etc and reaches a whole new television audience. Future showings will continue to command large fees for years to come. Also, each of these new releases will be marketed with tie-ins – a soundtrack album, computer game, book, etc. Each release opens up new avenues for cross-marketing – or exploitation, if you prefer. It's a very well-oiled business, and it ensures that the shelf-life of the blockbuster movie is considerably longer (and more lucrative) than its major album equivalent.

What makes the above comparison even more interesting is the way in which the film industry has taken something that was initially seen as a threat to its very existence – home video – and turned it into an additional marketing tool. Pretty neat, huh? The movie business thrived by redeveloping its business model, incorporating video exploitation into that model and going out of its way to make the movie-going experience as pleasurable and unique as possible. There's a lesson for the music business in there somewhere.

Embracing internet technology and digital delivery has to be the way forward for the music industry, and after much deliberation it's beginning to look as if the majors are coming around to this way of thinking. Sony and Universal are pursuing plans to launch a joint flat-rate service, while Warner Music, BMG and EMI all broke the MP3 taboo last summer by announcing plans to license their catalogue for download in conjunction with "the enemy", MP3.com (after successfully suing them via the RIAA for breach of copyright first, of course). Naturally, MP3.com couldn't be expected to pay royalties to Warner, BMG and EMI every time one of their songs was downloaded for free and stay in business for long, so how did they make it work? In a word, subscription.

the subscription model

You may not expect to pay each time you download a song from the net (too cumbersome and too expensive), but you'd probably be more willing to pay a monthly subscription to your local ISP or music content provider for unlimited access to a vast catalogue of your favourite sounds. At the height of the Napster debate, some two-thirds of users polled by online researcher

Webnoize agreed that they would be prepared to pay $10 a month to use the Napster service. After all, it's no different to paying a monthly subscription to Sky in order to view your favourite movies. On this basis, the record industry – in conjunction with MP3.com (although this relationship is still in its early days) – looks like it's finally developing a model not unlike that adopted by the TV industry, by providing customers with access to back catalogue material ostensibly for free (while retaining the initial raft of customer purchases of new releases) and making money through web-based advertising and subscription revenue.

The phenomenal success of the music-file-swapping antics of Napster, Freenet *et al* signposts the way towards the "celestial jukebox", where the history of recorded music is available in its entirety from anywhere at any time for a flat fee. Jupiter Communications predict that, by 2005, subscription listening will overtake pay per downloads as the most popular way of experiencing music online.

Indeed, the subscription concept is already well established. MP3.com launched its Classical Channel in 2000 and EMusic started its EMusic Unlimited online music service, allowing users to download more than 125,000 digital tracks from artists including Bush, Green Day and, er, They Might Be Giants (and EMusic might have been giants if they'd been able to build from a more star-studded catalogue). EMusic took the legitimate route of licensing material from artists and record companies and stressing guilt-free MP3s as their unique selling point, telling their users, "You bought it, so the artists get compensated."

At around $20 a month, however, selling unlimited access to low-profile content is a difficult task. Nevertheless, ease of access and the "hidden" feel of paying by subscribing can alleviate these difficulties. EMusic put it thus: "This type of all-you-can-download service creates a unique consumer experience by making the content extremely convenient, while feeling free." Not an altogether different philosophy to the one which underpins our viewing of *Friends* every Friday night, is it?

downloading, streaming and webcasting

music for the masses

Delivering music in MP3 file format is but one of a plethora of options that are available. We're close now to the development of the new generation of mobile phones which will allow the transmission of digital music via satellite. Web-based digital broadcasts (webcasts) are becoming increasingly popular, particularly for live performances, which can be streamed to several countries simultaneously around the globe. Pay-per-listen internet radio will soon be leaving hundreds of disc jockeys trailing in its wake. Any DJ worth his or her salt will be hosting web-based radio broadcasts and live simulcasts before too long – indeed, many already are – and downloading in MP3, Liquid Audio, Windows Media Audio and countless new file formats is helping take digital music to the internet-literate masses.

All of these different ways of delivering music open up exciting possibilities for artists wishing to communicate with new and bigger audiences – and, as this chapter will reveal, self-promotion is becoming increasingly viable as a result of new internet technology. The internet revolution also signals an upsurge in consumer power, providing music fans with unprecedented access to music of all kinds in a wide array of formats. The bedrock of the internet revolution, the selection of tools with which the internet is reshaping the music industry, are:

Downloads
Streams
Webcasts

Let's discuss how each works.

downloading music from the internet

Downloading is the mother of all internet activity, the lifeblood of internet music exploitation. It's a term that is used constantly, and means simply copying a file onto your computer in a permanent form. Downloading music from the net is the modern-day equivalent of (and now more popular than) taping a mate's album onto a cassette.

In January 2000, KNAC.com – the internet branch of the US hard-rock radio station – announced that its exclusive giveaway of Guns N' Roses' 'Coma' had generated 75,000 downloads in just three weeks. Several interesting things come out of this: it shows how a radio station that originally broadcast from Santa Monica to a Californian audience of rock fans can now suddenly reach air guitarists the world over; it shows that downloading (particularly if the artist is well known) is becoming very popular; and it shows that the download doesn't have to be in MP3 format to be successful (the track was available on the site in Microsoft's Windows Media format). Incidentally, 'Coma' didn't appear on Geffen's recently released Guns N' Roses live album – fans found the song only on the Japanese version of the record or through KNAC.com's exclusive download. This is the direction in which the record industry is increasingly moving.

let's get downloaded

"We're gonna have a good time. We're gonna have a party. Let's go…"
– Primal Scream

Er, well not quite. I'll let you into a little secret: downloading music from the internet is very, very easy, and at the moment is about as much fun as watching paint dry. Or golf. When BT finally decides that it's the right moment to roll out its ADSL lines, and when broadband access becomes standard, both the speed of downloading music and its quality will improve dramatically.

For now, though, once you've found a track that you want to download in MP3 format, all you have to do is click on the link marked "download now", or some such command, and sit back and wait for ten to 15 minutes. Once your computer's download manager tells you that the song has successfully transferred to your computer, you just have to open your MP3 player and click on Play to start the track playing. It's so simple that a seven-year-old child could do it (although not a 47-year-old record company executive).

So, the question for the net-friendly music fan is not so much "how do I download MP3s?" as "where do I go to find MP3s to download?". Now, this is where things get a little controversial. You can take two routes: the legitimate and the not so legitimate. The latter involves obtaining free copies of your favourite artists' songs from pirate web sites and "file-sharing" software applications, the most popular of which are Napster and Freenet.

where to find MP3s

What Is Napster?

For those of you who went into millennium hibernation and missed most of 2000, Napster is the most prominent of several controversial software applications that allow you to search the internet for MP3 files which match your specified criteria. For example, if you're interested in 1970s progressive rock (and, lets face it, who isn't?), you can type in specific band names (Yes, King Crimson, etc) or search by genre – for example, by typing in "progressive rock". MP3 files contain not only the music but also details of the artist, record company, track duration and all kinds of interesting information about the track in question on what's known as the ID3 tag, which enables Napster to select the MP3 files relevant to you. It has a phenomenal archive to choose from because, unlike other MP3 web sites, Napster doesn't actually store any of the files itself. Instead, it acts as a conduit, allowing users across the globe to access each other's private collections. Lawyers refer to this process as "peer-to-peer networking". By this, they mean that users are swapping their MP3 files from one PC (or "peer") to another, without the need to go through a central server. The point is, MP3 files are neither stored on, nor downloaded from, the Napster servers. (This is an important distinction, as we'll see later.)

What Is Freenet?

"Freenet screws the established music industry by making copyright laws unenforceable. I believe that's no bad thing."
– Ian Clarke, Freenet

Like Napster, Freenet is an electronic file-sharing software application which allows users to freely swap music files (in MP3 format) over the internet. Unlike Napster, Freenet's complex remote server program allows those swapping the files to remain anonymous. This is why it's so feared by the music industry, because it means that mass copyright infringement could take place on Freenet without any chance of catching the perpetrators.

the great Napster debate

Are Napster and its clones devaluing music? Or are they leading people to discover and purchase CDs by artists that they wouldn't otherwise have taken a chance on? It depends on who you ask: Metallica's Lars Ulrich or Limp Bizkit's Fred Durst. More specifically, is Napster acting illegally by providing the software that enables MP3 music files to be freely downloaded without paying the copyright owners? This question, among others, has been occupying the minds of the US District Court's judges of late.

the RIAA vs Napster

In the year leading up to the publication of this book, Napster's producers have been locked in a legal conflict with the RIAA (the Recording Industry Association of America, the same body which unsuccessfully tried to prevent the sale of the Rio, a portable MP3 player). The RIAA's argument is that Napster facilitates piracy by enabling and encouraging users to share MP3 files that they have already downloaded onto their hard drives. The problem is that many of these files have been downloaded illegally, without payment to the copyright owners. In the RIAA's words, Napster "has created a haven for music piracy on an unprecedented scale".

The RIAA are therefore asserting "contributory" copyright infringement by Napster. Remember, the MP3 files in question aren't stored on Napster's servers, so the RIAA can't sue for "primary" infringement of copyright. Were the infringing material to have been stored on Napster's servers, it's likely that Napster would have alleged that it is a service provider. ISPs can escape liability for illegal material held on their servers – a "safe harbour" – if they respond appropriately to complaints of infringement. However, such an argument would be unlikely to succeed, as Napster's service is unlike an ISP's because it connects users *through* the internet rather than connecting users *to* the internet, and therefore cannot be clearly said to be acting as an intermediary.

The initial court ruling (given by district judge Marilyn Hall Patel) – that the major record companies and publishers represented by the RIAA be granted a preliminary injunction against Napster – was therefore encouraging for the worldwide record industry, as it was the first time that there had been a court ruling determining that the copyright rules that apply in the real world also apply in the virtual (online) world.

Napster now has a disclaimer on its site, in the usual wording, warning users that they must not breach copyright and that they are responsible for the files. Yet the extent to which a site – the very existence of which is built on the premise that listeners want access to MP3 files without paying for them – can abdicate responsibility for the consequences simply by issuing a disclaimer is highly debatable, to say the least. After all, the people behind Napster must know that the majority of the MP3 files accessed through their site are going to be illegal. Why else would anyone visit the site if they could get the material direct from the artist's web site or from the artist's official record company site? These sites are easy enough to find, after all.

Still, regardless of the eventual outcome of the RIAA suit (which was still pending at the time of publication), if Napster is forced to cease operations there is nothing to stop it simply relocating its servers to another jurisdiction while the RIAA struggles to enforce its US judgement overseas.

Napster fallout

One of the interesting things about the Napster case was the reaction of the powerful technology industries to Judge Patel's initial ruling. They argued that Judge Patel had been wrong to issue Napster with an injunction, on the basis that such a ban would irreparably harm the growth of the internet. Summing up the apparent dichotomy in the ruling, the Digital Media Association (a US trade body representing Liquid Audio and AOL, among others, and one of many organisations to file briefs with the court) put it thus: "The whole backbone of the internet is available for copying. Does this mean that the internet could be illegal?"

Both AOL and Sony Electronics were among the firms criticising Judge Patel's decision, yet both are affiliated to the very record companies suing Napster. If nothing else, the Napster case was responsible for creating conflict within those multimedia corporations that own both record companies and technology firms. It's also true that the high-profile media attention attracted by the RIAA litigation gave Napster publicity and exposure for which it could not have paid.

Indeed, as the Napster debate raged in the wake of the RIAA's attempt to shut the service down, so support for pro-Napster factions flourished. A poll of over 2,000 internet music addicts taken by Jupiter Communications revealed that users of file-swapping music services such as Napster were nearly 50% more likely than non-users to increase their spending on music. The key, it seems, is that Napster users are music fans, after all. Indeed, in most cases, they're more than just fans – they're fanatics. They'd have to be to spend hours wired to the net, downloading songs 20 minutes at a time. As a form of music promotion, leading people to discover new albums by artists that they probably wouldn't risk forking out £15 on, Napster actually takes some beating.

The bottom line is that, if Napster increases CD sales, the record industry is going to be interested in harnessing the file-swapping technology in a legitimate way. Napster's co-founder Sean Parker said that he initially intended to use free music to "leverage the record companies into a deal". Now a subscription service run in partnership with the major labels seems to be the only way forward.

Indeed, in the lacuna that followed Napster's successful appeal against the original US District Court ruling, that the service should be shut down, and with Napster settling out of court with the majors, the major record labels worked feverishly to kick-start a legitimate market for digital downloads of named artists' repertoire. The chance – the "window of opportunity", as Jay Berman, head of the IFPI put it – was quickly grasped, and BMG, Warner and EMI all quickly entered into licensing agreements with MP3.com, allowing users to legally download major-label content from MP3.com for the first time. By the end of the year, all of the major labels had arrangements in place for the downloading of content in secure and non-encrypted MP3 format. Indeed, several of these arrangements bore more than a passing resemblance to Napster's file-sharing technology.

BMG, indeed, went one step further by entering directly into talks with Napster with a view to creating a joint file-sharing MP3 service, offering legitimately acquired tracks for download. The BMG/Napster alliance is still in its formative stage, but it seems inevitable that the Napster service will no longer be free to use.

legally downloading MP3 files

So, if you want to legally download MP3 files, there are now plenty of different options available. Aside from looking up major record labels' web sites directly (see Appendix II for a run-down of all of the significant record companies' web site addresses) or going to the MP3.com site, you can also enter "MP3" in your search engine to search for web sites which are likely to contain MP3 files. If you don't have an MP3 player at this stage, don't worry because most web sites will ask you if you need an MP3 player and will give you the opportunity to download one for free.

There are also numerous unsigned music web sites around that offer free downloads of music by unknown or up-and-coming artists, as well as a few who have seen better days. Finally, several MP3-dedicated sites, such as MP3now and Getoutthere and search engines such as Lycos ("MP3 Search"), have now launched specialist search facilities to help fans locate MP3 files on the internet.

uploading music onto the internet

how to create your own MP3 files

Before you can upload a song onto the internet, you first need to transfer it into a digital file format capable of being understood by your MP3 software. This process is known as *ripping*, which is not quite as exciting as it sounds. In fact, it refers to a process of digital audio extraction. To create MP3 files, you need to use a program known as an *encoder*, such as Audio Catalyst, Audiograbber or MusicMatch Jukebox. These are software programs that allow you to insert an audio CD in your computer hard drive and convert it into a set of MP3 files on your hard disk.

This process involves two stages: first the digital information is converted into a .WAV file, capable of being read by your computer; then the file is encoded into MP3 format. Fortunately, most encoders take care of both stages of this process. You can also create MP3 files from cassettes, simply by connecting the cassette player to the soundcard on your PC via a jack lead.

streaming music from the internet

how does RealAudio streaming work?

Streaming can be a complex process to visualise. In particular, a lot of people have difficulty in differentiating between streaming and downloading. If you imagine streaming as being like water flowing continuously, you're halfway there. With streamed data, however, the data doesn't flow continuously but is broken into thousands of little packets using UDP (User Datagram Protocol). Your RealPlayer monitors the arrival of these packets at your computer, and when it can make sense of them it plays them back (a process known as *buffering*) so that what you're seeing or listening to appears to be continuous. Because of the way in which streaming works, RealPlayer actually begins playback before the whole file has been received by your computer. This means that the listener can hear a song in real time without having to wait for the whole song to download.

Streaming is similar to traditional forms of broadcasting, such as television or radio, except that it is obtained on demand (ie you decide when you want it to start). Downloading, on the other hand, will always result in a copy of the track – or whatever other data is downloaded – being stored on your computer's hard drive. Once the download is complete, you will then be able to listen to the track whenever you want.

why RealAudio?

RealAudio is multi-format (ie it will work on Macs, PCs, laptops and so on) and the established market leader for streamed audio. Anyone can download RealPlayer for free from RealNetworks' RealAudio web site, located at http://www.real.com. RealNetworks make their money by charging people for the right to broadcast over the internet, granting development licences for a one-off fee. Almost everyone wanting to broadcast wants to do so using RealAudio because almost everyone in their potential audience will have a RealAudio player, which they'll have downloaded for free!

Streaming can complement downloading very well. Artists will be able to take advantage of its preview abilities by allowing fans to listen to RealAudio-streamed audio clips of MP3 files that they're considering downloading before doing so, simply by clicking the Instant Play link on the artist's site. Remember that downloading a five-minute song can take between ten and 20 minutes using a standard 56kbs (kilobit-per-second) modem, so the instant streaming option is a very useful way of previewing material before you take the plunge.

webcasting music on the internet

In October 1999, The Charlatans celebrated the release of their first major label release, *Us And Us Only*, with a midnight gig at HMV's Oxford Street store. The gig also marked the full "hard launch" of HMV's online store, and the band's performance was webcast live on the HMV.co.uk site by Virtue Interactive. It was a pivotal moment, the traditional album launch working hand in hand with a burgeoning new technology to take music promotion to a new level.

what is webcasting?

Webcasting is an internet technology that allows you to watch and listen to live (or later) transmissions of live events on your home computer. It's really a form of streaming, only with visual information streamed as well as audio. In time, news and sports networks, in particular, will embrace webcasting as a prime method of delivering sought-after events to consumers. The next time premier league TV rights go out to tender, the right to show live or edited highlights of matches on the internet will form a significant part of the package for broadcasters.

For the music industry, webcasting is already very big business. Music and the internet is truly a marriage made in heaven. The potential for live music events to attract traffic to web sites is phenomenal. Also, so many fans want to attend concerts but only a limited number of tickets are available, and only those few who live near enough are able to go. The next best thing is to sit back and enjoy the concert as it happens from the comfort of your living room.

how does webcasting work?

Audio and video feeds taken from the mixing and video production desks at the concert that is being webcast are run into several PCs onsite. The data is then encoded into the standard streaming formats (RealAudio and Windows Media Audio) and sent out to the internet via an ISDN line. The webcaster's servers then rebroadcast the information to the consumer's home PC. Ensuring that a webcast is successful is still an art form in itself, as a sufficient number of servers have to be set up in order to cope with the anticipated demand of the webcast and enough bandwidth has to be hired in order to contend with the servers' capacity for data transmission.

One option for webcasters is to multicast an event, which involves building other links into the webcast chain. This would mean them either linking up with ISPs around the world or building a network of their own. The advantage of multicasting is that it allows webcasters to get the stream as far as it can go before splitting it at the nearest point to its end destination. Using local ISPs means that the webcaster can increase the reach of the cast as well as the number of people who can log on simultaneously.

The standard reach of webcasting will improve massively in the next year or so. At the moment, though, there is still a bandwidth bottleneck in the "last mile" (ie the connection between a consumer's local telephone exchange and his home PC), and this will only be cleared by the full introduction of broadband internet.

webcasting live music

Webcasting represents an exciting new way for bands – both established acts and new, unsigned bands – to perform live to a potentially huge audience. Paul McCartney's Cavern Club gig in October 1999 was viewed by an estimated internet audience of 1,000,000. Just one year later, Madonna's Brixton Academy comeback gig, webcast by Microsoft, was viewed by an estimated nine million fans around the globe (although many complained of the poor audio-visual quality of the transmission). As the technology improves, enabling more people to log on at any given time, so webcasting will grow in importance.

Musicians can use webcasting to help their careers in several ways:

- Webcasts are a good opportunity to air new material to fans in the run-up to a release;

- Webcasts increase a live audience and can help stimulate sales of merchandise, as well as generate income in their own right;

- Live events on the internet are very popular with advertisers because they act as a focus and pull people in, and webcasters can consequently cash in on potential sponsorship or advertising revenues;

- For a new act, a webcast represents an excellent opportunity to get yourself seen by A&R scouts, as well as potential fans.

burning CDs

Another new form of digital copying of great interest to internet users is CD burning, particularly as it enables them to transfer their downloaded MP3 files to disk. CD burning is good fun – you'll find the lure of concocting home-made CD compilations culled from your record collection hard to resist. My particular favourite hobby is rewriting history by removing dodgy tracks from classic albums – *Houses Of The Holy* without 'The Crunge' and 'D'yer Mak'er' is much cooler, if considerably shorter.

CD burning is also very easy. All you need in order to rearrange the good works of Page, Plant and co is a piece of equipment known as a CD writer. CD writers allow you to create your own CDs (from MP3 files, for example) and – depending on the type you buy – erase and rewrite audio data onto disk. (See Appendix I for a list of the most popular models.) The vast majority of models allow you to store a maximum of 650MB or 74 minutes of data on each disk.

custom CDs

Following on from CD burning – and also utilising CD-burning technology – is the concept of paid-for custom CDs. Custom-created CD compilations are going to become a real feature of music stores and online music sales in the very near future. Their big attraction is that they give music fans the opportunity to create their own compilation albums from a variety of acts. Pre-chosen compilations are already massive sellers, particularly in the dance and pop arena, including the *Now That's What I Call Music* series, the *Cream* and *Ministry Of Sound* mix compilations, and not forgetting our old fave *Greatest MOR Rock Ballads*, featuring several over-blown guitar solos and production values so stodgy that they make Céline Dion sound cutting edge!

With custom CDs, you can skip the inevitable Lightning Seeds filler and line up a selection of corkers to make your party go with a swing. At least, that's the idea. At the moment, the choice for creating instore custom compilations is still fairly limited. London's market leaders – HMV's flagship new Oxford Street store, Tower and Virgin – have all now installed custom CD kiosks, but none are able to offer consumers more than 500 tracks at present.

Currently, the leading instore kiosk manufacturers are Chemistry, who use Liquid Audio software to enable customers to compile their own ten-track CDs, burning their personal selection onto CD within around ten minutes. Artwork for the CD can also be printed there and then. Chemistry have successfully engineered deals with BMG and several well-known independent labels, including Beggars Banquet, Ministry Of Sound, V2 and Telstar.

wireless application protocol

WAP is the future of human communication, or so the marketing men would have us believe. WAP will change the way we view the media and extend internet use to the mobile community. Grandiose though such ideas may seem, technology has the capacity to make this happen, and will be even better placed to do this when third-generation mobile phones hit the market in 2002.

WAP mobile phones are designed to work on all kinds of digital wireless devices and on all wireless networks. In the short term, this means that WAP will allow us to connect to the net via our mobile phones, thus rendering the home PC redundant as a means of accessing the internet. No, really, although quite why anyone would want to read web-page text on a tiny mobile phone screen is beyond me. Still, WAP does offer exciting possibilities for music on the internet:

• WAP will allow people to listen to music (samples and complete songs) streamed from the internet anywhere and at any time;

- WAP will enable labels, distributors and music web site operators to send out personally tailored text messages to fans about their favourite groups or pop news updates (such as the service now provided by the Genie/Worldpop alliance);

- WAP has the potential to turn bands into interactive multimedia artists by providing the means to disseminate visual images and interactive elements (ie fans performing their own remixes) together with the music anywhere in the world, at any time.

The major labels and distributors have been quick to climb on board. Last year alone, EMI, HMV and Startle (the UK's largest independent wholesaler) announced tie-ups with various mobile phone companies. Potentially, one of the biggest deals is the Startle/Vodafone agreement, which opens the door for some 200,000 titles to be either streamed as audio clips or downloaded. With Vodafone's takeover of German telecommunications giant Mannesman, subscribers to the Startle music and entertainment service could number up to 50 million!

WAP technology is still in development, but more up-to-date information can be gleaned from the online WAP browser at http://www.gelon.net.

the internet vs the record industry

the first MP3 superstar – what are the chances?

Is the internet likely to throw up its first MP3 superstar in the near future? Do we even want it to? Is that what the internet is all about? Creating and marketing a new MP3 superstar could be seen as the antithesis of everything that the internet stands for. Artist web sites – particularly unsigned music sites, such as Peoplesound and Vitaminic (which will be covered in the next chapter) – champion the idea that the internet is about democratising the process of becoming a superstar. They argue that music fans across the globe are now able to access all different kinds of music, so they can decide who they like and don't like, as opposed to a major label spending millions grooming and pushing a manufactured superstar onto the public, *à la* Mariah Carey.

micro-marketing

The obvious assumption is that the internet is perfect for reaching a mass-market audience – global marketing, a kind of ad man's dream. But just like pushing flyers through random letterboxes, this kind of scattergun approach is unlikely to achieve a high ratio of success. Instead, the clever money is on heavily targeting genre-specific audiences – micro-marketing, to use the industry vernacular. In an illustration of this approach, Chapter 8 looks at the success of the internet marketing campaign mounted by independent US label Wind-Up in support of the Christian rock band Creed, a kind of apotheosis of niche marketing.

The idea of superstars – a symptom of the mass marketing of things – is beginning to look out of date. Surely the real power wielded by a network with the ability to link music fans directly to their favourite band or label is the fantastic opportunity it gives even the smallest label or most cultish band to reach and target its fans. The internet is really best seen as a series of niche markets or micro-markets, reflecting the way in which the music industry seems to be developing and has been developing for the past five years – towards lots of different genres and sub-genres of music.

Since the demise of Britpop in the mid '90s, the UK music scene has fragmented to the point at which it's impossible to get a handle on a specific genre or movement. This is particularly the case with dance music, which can no longer simply be classified as, say, "disco" or "house". The current scene is a veritable smorgasbord of styles – hip hop, jungle, two-step, R&B, swingbeat, rap and so on.

Away from the dance market, you only have to take a look at the Mercury Music Awards nominations for 2000 for evidence of the increasing tendency shown by genuine artists to ignore trend and to concentrate instead on pursuing their own fragmented musical vision. The nominees were:

Coldplay: *Parachutes*
Badly Drawn Boy: *Hour Of The Bewilderbeast*
Kathryn Williams: *Little Black Numbers*
Doves: *Lost Souls*
Richard Ashcroft: *Alone With Everybody*
MJ Cole: *Sincere*
Nitin Sawhney: *Beyond Skin*
Death In Vegas: *The Contino Sessions*
Leftfield: *Rhythm And Stealth*
Helicopter Girl: *How To Steal The World*

A number of these releases (including the eventual winner, Badly Drawn Boy) were debuts, which is encouraging for the UK music industry. Even more encouraging is that few, if any, seemed to be tied to a rigid template or in awe of the past. The retrograde sound and song structures so beloved by Oasis have now given way to the pursuit of a more individual style. There are far more stars and far fewer superstars than ever before, and the internet is aiding this growth in the importance of local stars for local markets.

today's music scene – what's going on?

The music industry is changing at a rapid pace. Music is exploding into tiny segments, consumer loyalty is disappearing and big-name acts like REM and U2 can no longer count on fans to stick with them, while younger acts fear the "difficult second album" for commercial as much as for artistic reasons; record sales are declining in the face of stiff competition from other leisure industries (for example, are there any current pop stars as well known as David Beckham or Michael Owen?); there is an emerging preference for moods/styles/genres (compilation albums now account for a staggering 40% of album sales in the UK); the cost of launching artists is spiralling while more and more records are released each year (20,000 CDs were released in the UK in 1999 compared to 3,500 in 1989); and 95% of artists signed to record companies fail to give their labels a return on their investment (only 5% recoup and billions of dollars are written off in A&R each year).

Artists come and go very quickly in today's volatile and unstable climate. There is absolutely no guarantee that, just because your first album has been successful, the second will equal or better its success. The Bluetones, Embrace and Kula Shaker all debuted with chart-topping albums, but within a couple of years the zeitgeist had moved on and the follow-up albums went down the plughole. You can see the likes of Muse and Toploader going the same way.

Record companies need to be more scientific in their thinking. They can't afford to invest hundreds of thousands of pounds in an act and then watch them slip out of the charts quicker than you can say "*Onka's Big Moka*". The internet offers labels a chance to monitor and test-market new bands and to build data and obtain feedback before taking the plunge. Internet test-marketing is by no means a foolproof idea, but given the soaring cost of breaking new acts it's an opportunity that the record industry would be foolish to pass on.

A kind of Catch 22 situation has now developed in the marketplace: the newly-signed band has to cut commercial singles straight away and the label has to spend heavily on plugging and marketing. Radio 1 and the big commercial stations won't take a single by a new band seriously unless the label can show commitment to a big marketing spend, and this invariably means making a video in order to get a radio playlisting (logical, huh?), but in order to have the money to finance videos ideally you'll have had hits and broken onto the radio already. Then the label watches anxiously for the midweek chart position, and if their act is at, say, Number 35 they will probably invest even more money in sending buying teams out to ensure a Top 40 place in Sunday's chart. The single scrapes the Top 40 and then dives out the following week – and then the label has to start the process all over again for the next single…

It's a high-pressure environment, and the days of gradually nurturing talent away from the spotlight are long gone. It's impossible to believe that a band like Pink Floyd would have been allowed the opportunity to make albums like *A Saucerful Of Secrets*, *Atom Heart Mother* and *Meddle* before *Dark Side Of The Moon*. Today's Floyd would never have recorded *Dark Side*; they'd have been dropped long before, heavily unrecouped, or been forced to try and write some hit singles. EMI, in common with many of the major labels at the time, valued progression and understood that album bands needed to develop their writing over successive releases – they even created an imprint label, Harvest, for exactly those kinds of musicians, and did all they could to create an environment in which they could flourish.

While the industry remains obsessed with midweek chart positions, playlists and manufacturing boy bands, there seems to be little hope of things changing…unless and until the internet allows independent and creative artists and labels the chance to carve out their market share. But don't expect an MP3 superstar to come out of all this – the idea is as outdated as it is unlikely in an internet-music culture that encourages fragmentation and individualism. Still, do we really need another Westlife or S Club 7?

who decided that S Club 7 were going to be successful?

Actually, S Club 7 are an interesting case in point. They were as near as dammit guaranteed of superstardom before they had even released a record. Why? Because Simon Fuller's 19 organisation put the group together on the back of his phenomenal success with The Spice Girls. The boys and girls were hand-picked for their looks and their ability to perform move-perfect choreography routines during minor earth tremors. Hollywood decided to invest millions in a ratings-chasing TV series. Top producers and writing teams were hired to make sure that the songs – although marginally less important than the merchandising operation – had enough sugar-coated harmonies to be palatable to daytime radio. And, of course, the record label, Universal, decided to invest a few hundred thousand pounds on the marketing campaign. The 7 brand was launched with a calculated corporate strategy of Saatchi-esque proportions. Success was a self-fulfilling prophecy.

The point here is that there are a series of filters which enable the music-buying population to perceive the existence of certain records and not others. These filters are driven by the handful of large multinational corporations (Sony, Universal, AOL/Time Warner, EMI, BMG) that dominate the global music scene. One of the benefits that an organism like the internet is capable of providing in response to this globalisation is a different kind of filter system, a more altruistic set of filters that drive people to discover records other than those that they're told by the major record labels that they should discover.

Artists and music fans alike now have the opportunity to post and exchange lists of their favourite records on their web sites. The net is opening up access to all kinds of genres and styles of music, allowing music fans to choose who to listen to rather than be cleverly manipulated by a multi-million-pound promo campaign into listening to the same thing as everyone else.

There is a genuine two-way dialogue and interaction on the internet. A fan buys an album on the basis of reviews he's read on the net and then submits a review himself of a different record that he thinks other web users will like. Artist sites invariably request their fans' opinions of their latest records and, together with the unsigned and genre sites springing up on the net, invite listeners to vote with their feet (or perhaps that should be ears) by downloading the tracks that excite them.

It's the user or listener as reporter/artist/A&R man and the internet chat room as focal point of a global network for thousands of smaller music communities that makes the internet such an exciting alternative to the homogenised S Club 7 culture that would otherwise prevail indefinitely. The internet is going to play a big part in enabling good musicians with something interesting to say to build a career through developing a loyal niche or micro fanbase across the world. Whether this music world will exist on an underground level or whether any of these artists will cross over with major-label backing into the mainstream is not important.

the internet is getting artists thinking

"I'm leaving the major label system…It's a radical time for musicians, a really revolutionary time…If the majors aren't going to do for me what I can do myself…which is to drive millions of people to my web site in less than a month and provide real content for that web site, then they can go to hell…"
– Courtney Love on the Hole web site and her split from Geffen

In the wake of the Napster/MP3 debate, more and more artists are coming out in public and criticising their record labels (or, more pertinently, ex-record labels). The industry hasn't seen such an outcry since George Michael took Sony to court and Prince attended the Brit Awards with the word "Slave" inscribed on his face. (Incidentally, the unassuming, quiet-one-at-the-back drummer from Blur, Dave Rowntree, attended the following year's Brits with the word "Dave" across his face in exactly the same style. Well, you had to be there, I guess.)

The point is that the internet has got artists thinking about the ownership of rights and the ability to distribute and promote their own music. It's the very same issue that underpinned George Michael's anger with his contract with Sony: if the artist ends up paying for all of his recordings, how come he doesn't own his own masters? And if his record label don't want to take his latest album seriously enough to promote properly, why is the artist stuck in limbo, unable to do anything about it?

The latter concern, in particular, was at the root of a powerfully worded essay by The The frontman Matt Johnson. The letter – an open attack on his record label, Interscope-Universal – was posted on his web site, at http://www.thethe.com. The points raised by Johnson are interesting because they demonstrated the extent to which, by 2000, even reasonably well-known artists were already beginning to see the coming of the internet as a saviour, a way out of the corporate maze. "As Universal/Interscope seem either incapable or unwilling to distribute and promote my album properly," he wrote, "and as they've refused to give it back to me, then I've been forced to consider alternative ways of reaching my audience." One of the alternative ways that Johnson was looking for was the internet. Although unsure about the implications of making his music freely available for download, Johnson reasoned that this was the only way that he could get in touch with his fans and make them aware of the record's existence, so he released the album one track at a time on a weekly basis as MP3 files via his web site.

The never-ending Napster debate also sparked vociferous criticism of the mainstream record business from rock stars quick to point out the edge that MP3 was bringing back to the music scene. At the forefront, inevitably, were rock's dysfunctional couple, Billy Corgan and Courtney Love. Corgan allegedly supervised the release of a brand-new Smashing Pumpkins album, *Machina II/Friends And Enemies of Modern Music*, released onto the net in MP3 format via the Pumpkins' online fan community. The move was viewed as a direct riposte to the band's former record company, Virgin, who were said to have rejected some of The Smashing Pumpkins' latest material. (The band had parted company with Virgin a few months previously.) Meanwhile, in a diatribe against her former label, Geffen, Love declared, "I'm not threatened by Napster. I'd rather have 100 million people hear a song than less than a million through the old-school distribution system." Talking of the old-school distribution system…

what are the major record labels up to?

keeping out the gatecrashers

So, what are the major record companies doing in the face of all this artist criticism and the inexorable rise of the internet? Well, they're busy making themselves even bigger and more powerful by buying each other up and getting into bed with the likes of AOL and MP3.com.

Until the breakthrough AOL/Time Warner merger, announced in January 2000, the record industry had tended to come across as reactive in its thinking. The industry can't afford to sit back; it only increases the danger that the big telecommunications companies, ISPs and electronic hardware manufacturers – who know nothing about nurturing and developing young bands and still less about marketing and promoting music but who see the internet as a great opportunity – will muscle in and build their own power bases. That said, AOL were warmly embraced by Warner, but of course it can be better to work in conjunction with your potential competitors rather than against them.

boardroom blitz

The record industry's ability to manipulate the internet rather than be manipulated by it – to turn it into a successful medium of communication, marketing and distribution – will depend on its capacity to be more pro-active in its development strategy. This could be through strategic alliances with software and telecommunications companies; major publishers stockpiling copyrights; building an intra-industry internet presence, such as a global music portal; or through a combination of some or all of these. Inevitably, much of the decision-making and planning is flowing from the United States, where new media and record companies' new media policies are considerably more developed than their European counterparts.

Ultimately, for the majors, who can fall back on a rich back catalogue of copyrights and titles, the way forward looks to be alliances with the right partners (if the deals give them enough say in the running of the joint ventures). ISPs want content, and this gives Warner, EMI and the others considerable bargaining power.

For the vast majority of independently funded labels, however, the key may be to hive off or outsource those elements of their business that can be handled more effectively and economically by specialist concerns, such as database providers and fulfilment companies. Hand in hand with this strategy, independent labels will pursue licence agreements – either individually or collectively, through a representative body such as AIM – with the market-leading "e-tailers" and digital distributors limited to the right to download or compile tracks on custom CDs. (The best way for indies to achieve this is covered later.)

getting into bed with MP3.com

First they sue them, then they become best buddies and do deals together! The deals that BMG, Warner, Sony and EMI struck with MP3.com represented a watershed in the growth of online music. (All of the majors agreed licences with MP3.com, apart from Universal, who successfully sued them for damages estimated at around $118 million.) From the majors' point of view, it demonstrated their respect for MP3.com's business model, although these deals also highlight a lesson well learnt from real-world music licensing: when staking out new territories overseas, it pays to make a deal with the biggest pirate and then turn them into a legitimate adjunct to the label's business.

From MP3.com's perspective, these deals were all about content. In effect, MP3.com were saying, "We can't make our own business idea work without the support of the traditional players." No question, MP3.com needed major artist content to drive traffic to their site.

major label tactics part I: mergers

In the age of internet entrepreneurs (trustafarians, City types with pots of money and a desire to invest it in the glam and exciting world of "young people"), the majors were slow in positioning themselves to take advantage of the internet's business potential. However, maybe they were wise to weigh up their options carefully. After all, the "dotcom" bubble – fuelled by trustafarians, City types with pots of money, etc – burst months ago.

The haze is beginning to clear now, the bodies can be seen strewn across the battlefield, and out of the confusion, why, I could have sworn that there used to be five majors. The major labels are swallowing each other whole. It's been almost impossible to keep up with the corporate shenanigans, so let's refresh our memories.

The newly-created Universal Music Group merged with Seagram International. AOL merged with Time Warner, who in turn spent most of 2000 attempting to merge with EMI Publishing. While all of this was going on, Roger Ames, CEO of Warner, was concluding a deal to sell London Records to Warner Music International. Within weeks, EMI Music had announced their proposed tie-up with Warner. Universal/Seagram then detailed plans for a new-economy merger with French company Vivendi. Meanwhile, BMG plans to sell its 50% stake in AOL Europe by 2002, raising several billion pounds for an acquisition in the process. And it now appears that, with the Warner/EMI merger falling through, BMG have set their sights, firstly, on EMI. All will no doubt be revealed in due course…

the AOL/Time Warner merger

The fallout from the proposed AOL/Time Warner/EMI deals is still to be truly felt by the music industry. One thing looks pretty certain, though: if you take major broadband internet and cable access, add a wealth of copyright material from Madonna to Led Zeppelin and stir in a few million internet subscribers, you should have a recipe for success. Online music sales haven't really taken off yet, but the AOL/Time Warner merger could be about to kick-start the legitimate internet music revolution. The MP3 revolution, of course, is already well under way.

For the internet distribution of music to become as much a part of our life as hot-footing it to the local Our Price (or should that be V-Shop?) to buy the new REM album, three key elements will have to come together:

Content
Delivery Service
Customer Base

All of these elements are present and correct in the AOL/Warner deal. Warner obviously has the content (although not to the extent that it would have done if the merger with EMI Music had been given the go-ahead from the European Commission). It also has access to high-speed downloads via the broadband connections through its cable TV system. Meanwhile, AOL brings internet expertise and a customer base of 25 million internet subscribers to the party.

This is the first time that the record industry has had access to such a vast number of internet users. Warner has stolen a march on its rivals, but so too has AOL, as AOL can now target Warner's expansive music catalogue in a way that other ISPs can't. And unlike the catalogue some of the other digital distributors are busy acquiring, the Warner catalogue is well known to music fans. All that's needed now is a secure method of delivering that catalogue, and of course the go-ahead from the anti-trust concerns.

major label tactics part II:
partnerships and alliances

Alan McGee reckons that the internet will leave the majors redundant within ten years. Unsurprisingly, this isn't a view shared by the majors.

Increasingly, the major record companies will consider partnerships and joint ventures (rather than just licensing rights) as a key part of their online strategy. Hedging their bets, EMI recently bought shares in both a digital distributor and a custom CD operation (a 1% stake in Liquid Audio and a 40% shareholding in Musicmaker.com). Dwarfing these initial forays into the online marketplace, EMI's next moves were to enter into negotiations with Time Warner – and then, when the European Commission put the kybosh on those plans, with BMG – to create the biggest music content provider for the internet in the world. Universal Music, meanwhile, have entered into partnership with InterTrust to offer the secure digital delivery of music, and recently launched its "bluematter" digital format, making tracks by major artists available for download for the first time. And Sony have been engaged in talks with Microsoft to use Microsoft's Windows Media technology to post singles from top artists such as Lauryn Hill and Fatboy Slim on internet sites for customers to download for about the same price as that of CD singles in shops.

Flexibility in marketing and promoting acts is also a factor. In the US, a Mariah Carey single released in 1999 was offered for download by Microsoft using their WMA software, promoting both their Windows Media Player and the artist simultaneously – a useful contribution to Sony Music's marketing budget for the release. And Sony didn't stop with simply offering downloads; in the latter part of 2000, having successfully sued MP3.com for building a digital audio library using copyright material, Sony proceeded to set up its own streaming music service using similar methods. Known as a *digital locker service*, the concept is indeed similar to MP3.com's MyPlay, enabling users to store videos, songs and images in a virtual web-based space.

major label tactics part III:
music portals

A music portal is internet-speak for the presenting of a music-based shop-front on the web. A portal is more than just a web site, however; it encompasses a whole range of processes and working parts. In the context of the major record companies (and also, in fact, several indies who were co-opted into the discussions), the idea of a music portal was developed to set up a jointly-owned and -funded venture which would enable fans to buy, listen to and download music, merchandise, concert tickets and so on from a cross-section of genres.

how would a music portal work?

Effectively, the portal would be a kind of enormous, online shopping mall. Behind the scenes, the "back-end" functions – such as the maintenance of catalogue and customer databases, the processing of credit card transactions and the fulfilment of orders – would be carried out by dedicated, possibly non-music-industry organisations. On the shop-front (the fans' point of contact with the portal), a glittering array of product would be available for purchase, including new releases and back catalogue from all of the major labels. The portal would be linked to numerous other web sites – artist sites, specialist music sites (eg the Top Of The Pops site). Ultimately, the portal would become established as *the* place to shop for music on the net.

Well, that's the idea in theory. In reality, the idea of a music portal is still a possibility but an unlikely one. For a start, the independents were never going to be keen to participate in a jointly-shared infrastructure where front-end space (ie the front pages of the web site) were likely to be dominated by major-label releases. Indeed, even the majors couldn't agree on how the editorial content was going to be divided. And besides, they were all too busy working on their own individual plans and strategic partnerships to pay more than lip service to the idea of a communal venture.

The record industry is very competitive. To succeed in this project, it would have to work a little like the airline industry, where all of the major airlines are prepared to send their pricing and ticket information to central computers for travel agents to access, despite being in direct competition with one another. This, of course, raises a number of questions. How would the labels go about pricing their releases? Would the portal end up with a consistent offer to the customer? Would the portal be able to accept money from an individual label to advertise its releases ahead of others? What of the legal issues – collective pricing, in particular – with regard to the record industry working together?

The difficulties in answering these and many other questions satisfactorily make the chances of there being a global music portal a long shot at present.

major label tactics part IV:
the Madison Project

It sounds like something out of a Harry Palmer spy thriller from the '60s – a distant relative of *The Ipcress File*, perhaps – although the reality is a little more mundane, if just as shrouded in secrecy and espionage.

The Madison Project aims to deliver albums over the internet, and the project involves the majors (EMI, BMG, Sony, Universal and Warner) working in conjunction with IBM to develop a secure method for downloading and digitally distributing music over the internet. Trials started in San Diego in 2000, limited to subscribers to Time Warner's Roadrunner cable modem. At the time of publication, the project still had to be rolled out into any other territories, so as yet there is little evidence to suggest that this will prove a viable alternative to delivering music in MP3 format.

what are the major music publishers up to?

Although these days music publishers such as EMI Music, Warner Chappell, BMG *et al* have a lower profile than their record-company counterparts, the internet revolution is affecting the publishing industry every bit as much as the record industry. As the owners of copyrights in songs, publishers also stand to lose if widespread pirating of copyrighted music continues. And as with their record-manufacturing siblings, publishers must also view the internet not as a threat but as an opportunity to make music available to a wider audience.

internet opportunities...

The major publishers are busy hoarding and buying up copyrights to strengthen their hand in the changing market. (Witness Universal Music Group's $400 million purchase of Rondor Music and EMI's acquisition of large swathes of Hit And Run Music and Windswept Pacific's catalogues in recent months.) Ownership of copyright is now seen as the key element in any music portfolio. Why? Simply because, as long as people pay to broadcast or consume music, publishers will get paid.

Publishers are less dependent on the form that this music distribution takes than record companies, who are justifiably concerned that a decline in physical distribution will lessen the hold they exert over their artists. On the other hand, they know that the MP3 revolution will lead to a broadcasting explosion across the globe.

Although income derived from record sales (*mechanical royalties* – see below) will see little increase as the market for pre-recorded music remains static or falls away, internet radio, streaming, webcasting, downloading and digital TV and radio will all create new broadcasting and performance revenue streams for publishers. Global link-ups, in particular – such as Net

Aid or Madonna's Brixton Academy live webcast – represent a tremendous opportunity for boosting performance income.

With that said, however, mechanical royalties still represent publishers' biggest slice of income (approximately a third of their overall revenue), and the future of these is far from clear, as far as online exploitation is concerned.

...and challenges

For UK publishers, the key topic of debate is the drawing up of new pricing models with record companies which, in particular, allow for a proposed mechanical royalty rate of 10p per song in the UK for music downloaded from the internet (for a song five minutes long or less). Mechanical royalties are those paid by record companies and, as we'll see in Chapter 12, by online radio stations, for the right to reproduce songs on record and to upload music onto the internet.

The proposed 10p rate is controversial, as publishers argue that the growth of the internet market makes it very uncertain who will be selling or distributing music in the future, while record labels think that 10p per song is too high a benchmark. The publishers' justification for setting such a rate is the need to establish a value for music used for online purposes. And, as I've pointed out in the context of record companies, online customers will choose which tracks they want and ignore others.

Normally, labels pay 8.5% of the price paid by retailers for a record. In the case of a single with a dealer price of, say, £1.80, this would equate to around 15p for three tracks. Given that most people are paying for the A-side, the publishers' proposed download rate does not appear to be unreasonable, particularly when you consider that, as online sales take off, record companies will benefit from seeing retail and manufacturing costs slashed. Nonetheless, the BPI and AIM (the record companies' trade associations) are fighting the 10p rate tooth and nail. It looks like we could have another Lewis vs Holyfield on our hands…

the Warner/EMI merger and EMI/BMG merger talks

"I believe in the music business. I liked it when there were five big players. I liked it even more when there were six…"
– *Walt Disney co-chairman Michael Eisner*

The timing of the proposed Warner Music/EMI merger – which came just a fortnight after the AOL/Time Warner tie-up had been announced –

shocked the music industry and further emphasised that the growth of online distribution was forcing the majors to seek security in consolidation. Unlike the AOL deal, which finally got the go-ahead from the US regulatory authorities in December 2000, the concern shown in Brussels over the "vertical integration" that would have resulted from Warner and EMI using AOL's 25-million-plus subscribers worldwide to distribute their music, leading to a possible stranglehold on the internet music market.

Following the collapse of the Warner/EMI deal, at the time that this book was published BMG and EMI were locked in talks with a view to creating the world's largest music company. It has been reported that BMG may have to sever its links with Zomba – enabling Zomba to stand alone as a fifth major – in order to gain clearance from anti-trust legislators.

Nonetheless, if the EMI/BMG deal does go through, the well-known labels EMI, Capitol, Parlophone, Virgin, Chrysalis, BMG, RCA and Arista will all be housed under one roof. Between them, these labels account for approximately a quarter of the global record market and a third of global music publishing sales. The merger will transform the content-ownership playing field at a stroke. All of a sudden, a huge stock of copyrights – from The Beatles to The Spice Girls to Moby to Whitney Houston – will be concentrated in the hands of one conglomerate.

Unquestionably, one of the most significant driving forces behind the EMI merger talks with both Warner and BMG is the inexorable growth of the internet. The music industry has suffered the ramifications of the internet revolution probably more swiftly and with greater force than any other global business. Music was ripe for the picking; from the moment it was first digitised, it became "content" to be squeezed down the world's phone lines and cables. Other comparable art forms – books, painting, movies, theatre and sculpture, for instance – aren't as malleable. Even in its physical form, music is the ideal size and shape for home-delivery e-commerce sales. Its unique importance in the Internet Age places invaluable store on its bedrock: content. The internet has transformed the importance of owning content beyond all recognition. The EMI/Warner/BMG talks are testament to this.

One of the record industry's biggest worries in the wake of the announcement of the original AOL/Warner merger was that AOL would use music as a loss-leader to drive traffic to its internet business at Warner's expense. Still, if EMI had come on board, it's very unlikely that the combined weight of the majors would have been prepared to let that happen, particularly as EMI's shareholders would have bemoaned the devaluing of the company's content while reaping none of the benefits of the original AOL/Warner joint venture.

All things considered, in the light of the increasing power of online service providers and telecommunications companies, the EMI/Warner deal would have been of wider benefit to the music business. As Robbie Williams's manager, David Enthoven, rather pithily put it on hearing of the proposed merger, "I wasn't surprised, but I'm delighted it wasn't Cable & Wireless they did the deal with."

…and if the EMI/BMG merger goes through?

"I always said indie or die, and now some of those people who aren't indie are going to die."
– Play It Again Sam's Kenny Gates

Inevitably, if a deal of these proportions goes ahead, there are going to be major ramifications for the industry, even if it takes time for these to be truly felt. Independents have already been quick to seize on the proposed merger as justification for remaining wholly independent and therefore in a prime position to fill the vacuum left by the disappearance of another major. Labels such as PIAS, Edel and Beggars Banquet can point to their policy of working in partnership with other pan-European independents and distributors as showing them in a more favourable light with artists. As V2's David Steele put it, "These big groups are going to have a lot of muscle, but new bands aren't interested in muscle; they want creativity. And you don't need to be a big company to do good A&R and marketing."

There is a second reason why well-positioned independent labels will now be able to attract artists of a higher calibre than before. These kinds of mega deals make artists nervous, and with good reason. With mergers of the EMI/BMG deal's proportions, it's invariably the case that a certain amount of "consolidation" or "rationalisation" of the business (as it is euphemistically known) will follow shortly after. In other words, artists will be dropped as the newly-merged venture examines ways of making savings and targeting its core sellers for investment. So although at first glance the EMI/BMG deal appears to be bad news for creativity and independence, it may well turn out to be the complete opposite. A merger of this size can often act as a catalyst to kick-start a new generation of indie labels into challenging the pre-eminence of the majors, not least in their ability to sign up quality artists.

will record stores still exist?

High Fidelity wouldn't have been half as entertaining if the focal point of the movie had been John Cusack sitting in his bedroom trawling the internet for obscure back catalogue to flog from his online music store. There isn't much social interaction involved in purchasing a record merely by clicking on an icon and without ever leaving your house. For Smiths and Cure fans in the mid '80s, the only time that they got to leave their black, bin-liner-covered bedsits during daylight hours was to purchase the latest vinyl offerings from their heroes. Record stores are a force for social good in the community. Of course they will continue to exist…won't they?

Alas, it's by no means cut and dried. The digital distribution of music represents a massive challenge to record shops, from our favourite independent stores in London's Berwick and Wardour Streets to the high-street megastores of Virgin and HMV. The internet signals the most powerful force for change that they have ever seen, a change that has already manifested itself in several ways:

- Traditional supply lines are being altered as MP3 technology allows record companies and artists alike to go direct to the consumer, with the consequence that the once-clear roles of record companies (to supply music) and record shops (to sell it) has become increasingly blurred;

- Sales of physical product are being increasingly hit by the rise of online distribution as faster, broadband internet connections and unmetered access become commonplace;

- Record companies are making product increasingly available for digital download from the net before it is released through retail (*à la* David Bowie's recent album, *Hours*), and at a cheaper price;

- Online distributors are narrowing the gap between staggered US/UK releases, undermining the lucrative import trade.

For music retailers, maintaining their central position in the marketplace as it undergoes rapid change is going to be a tough challenge.

The worst possible outcome of the online music revolution is an empty high street and retailers having to shut up shop. A future without traditional retail – is that a realistic possibility?

can music retailers survive?

Bricks-and-mortar retailers need to adapt quickly to the new trading environment and ensure that they benefit from the avenues that are being opened up. Music retailing has already survived home taping, copying and pirating, and it should – despite a sensationalist tone in media reporting over the past couple of years – survive the internet revolution. So far, music fans are pre-disposed to buy from retailers rather than direct from record companies. Customer attitudes, as well as the new technologies, remain largely untested. Still, there is a lot of hard work ahead for traditional music retailers if they wish to remain the music fans' first choice for buying music.

In particular, high-street retailers need to (a) embrace the internet as a means of expanding their customer base and (b) focus on how to differentiate the instore shopping experience from its online counterpart. Let's take each of these in turn.

online music retail

The internet provides retailers with a great opportunity for stocking deep (back) catalogue. The physical constraints of a high-street store disappear into the black hole of cyberspace, and virtual record stores have the ultimate luxury of being able to give the customer whatever he or she wants, provided that their fulfilment and restocking systems are in place. You want *Octoberon* by Barclay James Harvest? No problem. *Brain Salad Surgery* by ELP? It'll be my pleasure. *King Arthur On Ice* by Rick Wakeman? Ah, now you're asking.

Limitless catalogue is not the only great thing about online retailing. The opportunity to forge direct relationships with customers through online promotions and competitions and to monitor buying patterns by demographic (age, location, music taste, etc) will allow online record stores to target promotions at specific customers. For example, if I buy, say, *Highway To Hell* at Tower Records online, Tower will be able to e-mail me prior to the next AC/DC release and give me an exclusive offer available for online customers only – for instance, the chance to purchase the album with a discount/free poster/build-your-own replica Angus, complete with school uniform. The marketing possibilities are endless.

Online music retailers are in a strong position. Music is potentially a very big driver of traffic, in netspeak. As a result, there are plenty of other companies operating online that are very keen to hook up with and link to music retail sites. Entrepreneurs putting together lifestyle web sites (many aimed at the lucrative 18-30 market) view music as an indispensible part of the package.

In order to stay viable, traditional retailers should look to maximise all of these opportunities while simultaneously providing customers with an enjoyable instore shopping experience.

instore music retail

The role model for the record shop of the Digital Age is HMV's brand-new flagship store, which opened in London's Oxford Street in May 2000. The key for retailers is to make their record stores as high tech and as customer friendly as possible in order to make high-street shopping an enjoyable alternative to the online experience. The new HMV is the embodiment of this approach, which aims to provide the following:

- The physical experience of shopping for music showcased with catalogue information points – allowing customers to access the entire range of music that HMV have for sale through a database – and scan-based listening posts, enabling customers to preview albums quickly and effectively by scanning the relevant bar codes;

- A DVD cinema area with fixed screens and digital visual merchandising units showing everything from still images to video clips, emphasising the entertainment aspect of visiting the store;

- Sofas, cafes and book/magazine-reading facilities emphasising the social element of shopping;

- Burn-your-own custom CD kiosks allowing customers to compile their own albums from a wide range of tracks.

Not all independent record stores are going to be able to compete on this level, but key elements of old-style shopping (a face-to-face expert service for customers, instore promotions, attractively-laid-out stores, etc) combined with aspects of the new (CD-burning kiosks and cutting-edge stock, from DVDs to portable MP3 players) should ensure that traditional retailers retain their place in the supply chain.

chapter 5

musicians and the internet

> **T**he internet is saving the group, the artist, the songwriter and producer. Can you imagine the amount of product sat gathering dust, never released? It's back to the days when you cut a record one day and put it out the next."
> – Chuck D, Public Enemy

a life without record companies

What do you need record companies for? Do they have a God-given right to put out your records? Until recently, it always seemed that record companies were the only passport to making it in the music business.

Bands have always dreamed of getting signed up. Why else would they lug their gear down narrow staircases and play sweaty, beer-stained little venues to indifferent audiences, sometimes smaller in numbers than the band itself, were it not for the hope that an A&R talent scout was lurking somewhere in the shadows at the back?

You have to have a record deal, otherwise who's going to put out your records and make you a star? At least, who's going to hire the limo, pay the bill for the wrecked hotel furniture and pander to your every whim and fancy? Sure, on the one hand a life in the record industry is about glamour, freedom and untold debauchery, but it's also about making a living out of playing music – and selling records. And anyway, all that sex, drugs and rock 'n' roll stuff is *sooo* '90s!

Today, young bands are much more clued-up about the industry. They believe in their music, but they also appreciate the importance of getting a good deal and making the right commercial decisions. And these days,

62

decision number one is (or should be) whether or not you can go it alone, using the power of the internet to get your music out there. The short answer to this question is yes – possibly – but there are quite a few obstacles to overcome first.

the internet opportunity

In this chapter, we'll look at routes around these obstacles and other possible ways of bypassing the stranglehold that the traditional record company has on its artists' every movements. The chances are that you'll still need to have a contract with a label, but not necessarily on the same terms as those that labels are used to. The internet represents a big opportunity for musicians to claw back some of the immense power that the record companies have exercised over them for the past 50 years. It provides them with the opportunity to move towards greater independence from an industry that, to date, has enjoyed the exclusive right to fund, market and exploit musicians' recordings.

a traditional career in rock 'n' roll

Until now, bands have followed the same old well-trodden path. If you follow it too, your career in the music industry – if you're one of the very lucky few to get signed in the first place – will probably go something like this: play pub circuit endlessly; mail out demo tape to every record company on Earth; eventually get deal (if very lucky); sign away all rights (including those you didn't know you had); spend hundreds of thousands of pounds of record company money finding your "musical direction" and "image"; discover what you want to do – oh, too late, dropped after first album with unrecouped balance of quarter of a million; no other record company will touch you; career in window-cleaning beckoning.

Did I glamorise it too much?

do it yourself

The internet may help musicians to avoid this dismal scenario. How? Because the internet represents a way of staying independent. The less indebted you are to a record company, financially and morally (they can make you feel terribly guilty about all the money they're spending), the more chances you have of guiding your career where you want it to go. It's all about staying in control. To do that, you have to do as much for yourself as possible and/or keep hold of as many of your rights as you possibly can.

Put another way, what do record companies do that you can't do yourself? In the final analysis, there are three reasons why record companies exist:

- They advance money to artists in order to finance the cost of making recordings;

- They manufacture and distribute their records;

- They take away risk and market their records.

We'll take each part of this holy trinity in turn.

Making Your Recordings

It's now commonplace for artists to finance the cost of their recordings themselves. Home studio technology is very advanced, particularly for musicians using computers and software programs to record and mix their material (such as Pro Tools, Steinberg's Cubase and Audio Logic). It's true that, at the moment, artists involved in dance music are benefiting most from the new computer technology. If used intelligently and imaginatively, samplers can bring an entire orchestra of recorded sound into your music. DJ Shadow created the landmark *Endtroducing* album using just a sampler, a PC and a few outboard effects.

If you're a rock band, in technological terms you've begun to resemble a dinosaur. Rock bands need so much more space in order to rehearse, store their gear and wash their denim jackets. They're expensive to transport around, and capturing their music is harder and more demanding of expensive studio time and equipment, involving the use of valve microphones, multitrack reel-to-reels, reams of analogue and digital effects and so on.

Still, even guitar-based music is moving away from analogue recording processes as hard-disk recording gradually consigns 2" tape to the cutting-room floor. The Charlatans' first album for a major was also the first to be recorded on all digital equipment at their own Big Mushroom Studio, and Gomez managed to record their debut album in its entirety in their garage.

Even though it's drum and bass and, increasingly, hip-hop and R&B acts that are breaking through first as self-financed artists, it doesn't matter which musical genre sets the precedent. The point is that home-studio music is being recorded at pro-studio sound quality right now.

Manufacturing And Distributing Your Recordings

It remains pretty much impossible for you to take control of physically distributing your own records – unless you happen to own a fleet of Securicor vans and a large warehouse just outside Walsall. But that could all be about to change with the advent of online distribution. As MP3 and other, more secure formats of music become the primary medium of delivering music to people's homes, so you will be able take control of the distribution of your own material.

In the meantime, it's perfectly feasible to effect small-scale deliveries of CDs ordered from your web site and to build up a database of your fans from the orders and e-mails sent to it. When MP3 or the equivalent becomes the standard music format, you'll then be able to upload your music direct from the finished DAT or CD master and download an unlimited number of copies to your fans. You'll no longer need to rely on manufactured product in order to reach your audience.

By eliminating manufacturing and distribution from the equation, you are removing two of a record company's biggest reasons for existing. That said, physical product is still going to retain its importance in music – music fans will always want to own an actual record, whether on vinyl, CD, MiniDisc or whatever, together with the packaging, cover art and so on (and no, a graphic reproduction you can look at on your computer isn't the same thing). It's just that physical product and digitally distributed music will co-exist. You could fulfil the electronic orders for your music yourself, maybe in conjunction with a software company or maybe with your ISP. Meanwhile, you could strike a separate agreement with a manufacturing company and distributor to handle the physical sales of your music. There's no reason why it has to be a record company that undertakes all of these functions – unless, in a competitive marketplace, they are the people offering you the best deal.

Marketing Your Recordings

Marketing and promotion is one area in which record companies have a lot of experience. It's not just a question of fly-posting the country in the week before release or remembering to book the half-page advert in *NME*. Breaking a band is all about several factors coming together at once. Advertising is timed to coincide with features in the music press, which in turn are timed to coincide with the pre-release of the record to clubs, pluggers going to radio and approaching sympathetic producers, promos going out to journalists, live reviews published in the week before the single review appears, and so on.

Apart from the record company's obvious expertise in these areas, there is also the cost involved. Who else is prepared to underwrite the financial risk of turning you into a superstar? Marketing is a phenomenally expensive business. Singles generally don't make money; they are viewed by labels as loss-leaders, a promotional necessity paving the way to a successful album. It's not unusual for a label to spend £200,000 on a band that they really believe in, which would cover a couple of videos, a couple of UK tours, advertising, plugging and out-of-house PR – and that's just on the first two or three singles! And remember, we're only talking about marketing costs at the moment, not the cost of recording the album.

It's still feasible that you could sidestep record companies even here and hire specialist marketing firms to undertake your promotional work for you. Working in co-operation with other artists could possibly enable you to jointly fund a marketing team, but this option is a long shot at the moment. As long as they remain willing to take on the financial risk of marketing and promoting you, record companies still serve a valuable purpose in the recording supply chain.

the good will out

There is, however, the small matter of buzz, and no amount of carefully scheduled advertising is going to turn a dud into a hit. (I'm not referring to the manufactured boy-band/girl-group thing here – that operates on an altogether different financial plane.) A band that has people talking and is seen as hip will get music press coverage, and if they make a great record then people will play it.

So, the moral of the story is that, if you're in a great band, you don't necessarily need a big marketing spend – you'll make it anyway. You've also got a much better chance of making it on your own terms, and today that means using the internet and keeping hold of as many rights, in as many territories, as you can.

Think about any of the significant bands of the last ten or 15 years. Public Enemy, The Stone Roses, Nirvana – those bands made it on their own terms. If they were hyped, it wasn't orchestrated hype; it was genuine enthusiasm from music journalists. If any of these bands had been beginning their careers today, you can guarantee that they'd be pioneering internet use as a means of creating their own subculture, communicating with their fans and, as far as possible, disenfranchising the record companies. In fact, even now, ten years past their peak, Chuck D and

Public Enemy are leading the way with MP3-only releases (although cynics might argue that this is because they can't get their records in the stores any more).

What young musicians have to grasp is that MP3 and the internet is the start of an underground culture on a global scale. As we discussed earlier, MP3 and the internet have brought back the do-it-yourself ethos of the punk era and Chicago house scene. Just as in '76 and '86, the rules are there to be broken.

web-based success stories

Paul Brindley, the former bass player with early-'90s indie stalwarts The Sundays, points out in his excellent publication *New Musical Entrepreneurs* (available by e-mailing ippr@centralbooks.com) that there have already been some genuine go-it-alone success stories for artists prepared to work hard at self-promotion and develop eye-grabbing web sites. The unsigned acts in question – Silverman and Stargirl – have taken different routes in their attempts to reach and build an internet fan base.

London-based Stargirl's strategy has been to focus on their own web site as their window onto the online world rather than to hook up with the many unsigned music web sites currently touting their wares. (More on these later in this chapter.) Stargirl's Seb Lee-Delisle reasoned, "Unless they actively promote us, there really is no incentive." The band have taken great pains to design an impressive web presence of their own, offering free audio clips of their music as well as mail-order CDs and merchandise. The fact that they've sold over 4,000 singles to date – without recourse to record label, manager or publisher – is testament to their entrepreneurial skills.

Silverman, on the other hand, have been happy to embrace several of the unsigned music sites, including Peoplesound, MP3.com and Besonic. Despite having never performed live, they found themselves collecting an award from Streamsearch.com at Playboy Mansions in Los Angeles. Who said that there was no glamour in being in an unsigned band?

Still, going it alone remains, as yet, a tough option for even the most committed and web-friendly bands. We still need to see many more people on the net (particularly outside the US), much quicker net access and the endorsement of a few established stars before we get there. Reaching the mass market remains the key to making money out of music, and in order to do that…well, you need a little help from the guys with the big dollars to spend.

using the internet to get a record deal

The do-it-yourself route isn't going to suit everyone. Some artists will prefer the comfort and security of working within the structure of a traditional record company, while others will find that the internet helps them to build a loyal and dedicated fanbase but that turning this into substantial sales will require production and distribution of physical product. Even so, the internet could still have played a part in breaking that band.

So, here's another possible career route: get a record deal first, retain a degree of independence (ie own your own web site), limit the rights granted (which is becoming increasingly possible, as you'll see later in this chapter) and work in conjunction with the label to develop your career. Then hit paydirt and return to a (semi-) autonomous internet-led existence, communicating with your fans directly. But first, though, there's the small matter of actually getting the deal. The internet can help you in this, but you also have to do all of the obvious things which, being the sussed hep-cats that you are, you probably already know. But for those of you that don't, here's a brief list of dos and don'ts.

- **Do** record a demo tape and spend time and money getting it right. Put a maximum of three songs on it, and put the best song first. Which is the best song? Well, that depends on what kind of band you are, but usually either the most accessible or the most representative and, ideally, both;

- **Don't** spend ages on compiling some cheesy biography and moody band photos, and **don't** worry about mastering onto CD. Old-fashioned tape is best because (a) it shows that you aren't trying too hard and (b) it's very easy to skip tracks on a CD. If they're on tape, the A&R bod is more likely to give your song, oh, at least 30 seconds;

- **Do** attempt a bit of ligging. Find out the right names and, if you don't have a manager or well-connected friend to deliver the demo for you, try and hand-deliver it yourself or get your lawyer to play it to his A&R contacts;

- **Don't** send unsolicited tapes or CDs. They will go to the bottom of the pile and will probably never be heard;

- **Do** line-up a few gigs in the right places once the demo is complete, if you're a live band. Normally, only Monday-Thursday nights will attract slothful A&R types;

- **Don't** play any cover versions, unless they're obscure enough to get A&R people nodding their heads in appreciation at recognising such a cult track – it pays to flatter them!

how does the internet change things?

You should still follow the tried-and-tested rules above, but the internet does give you another string to your bow: it provides labels and artists with a new environment in which to meet one another. It's also a new way of winning exposure for your band and a chance to start selling your music before you've got a record deal. And currently the best way to maximise this exposure is to sign up with one or more of the web's record-company fly-traps: unsigned music web sites.

unsigned music web sites

"If thousands of people say that an artist is good, it's got to be worth looking at."
– Sas Metcalfe, EMI/Chrysalis A&R director

Note the following A&R rating system™:

***** John Lennon is miraculously reincarnated and arrives at record company offices armed with six albums' worth of previously undiscovered Beatles recordings;

**** Spend four hours rooting through tape pile and discover new Elvis Presley;

*** Spend four hours rooting through tape pile and discover new Elvis Costello;

** A cold, wet Wednesday spent travelling to Hull to see indie combo Gurn (influences: Shed 7 and Sleeper). Arrive to find gig cancelled after bass player strains plectrum finger in bizarre tour-bus Scrabble incident;

* A cold, wet Wednesday evening in Hull watching Gurn.

Peoplesound.com
Launched: November 1999
Software: MP3, RealAudio
Traffic (not the Winwood variety): 18,000 hits per day

Peoplesound.com is the web site with the most unsigned acts – in excess of 4,000, at the last count. This isn't necessarily a good thing, as the sheer volume of acts could dissuade A&R representatives from visiting. Nonetheless, the site does claim to enforce a strict A&R policy, so there must be a hell of a lot of good unsigned bands out there! Peoplesound is probably the best-known unsigned artist web site, mainly because it has adopted the most aggressive marketing strategy, spending heavily to promote the Peoplesound brand to consumers and offering all of its artists a £100 advance.

A&R Rating: **

Vitaminic.co.uk
Launched: September 1999
Software: MP3, RealAudio
Traffic: 20,000 hits per day

Vitaminic lets you create your own web pages and gets your music online in MP3 format. Like other unsigned music sites, Vitaminic isn't a record company but instead calls itself "a platform for promoting and distributing music". You can price the tracks that you wish to sell at your own discretion, but you must upload at least two free tracks for promotional purposes.

Recent developments have seen Vitaminic announce a tie-up with BMG in Italy and a launch in Sweden, helping to establish it as the first online distributor to offer localised content in different languages across Europe.

A&R Rating: ***

Musicunsigned.com
Launched: September 1999
Software: RealAudio (streaming only)
Traffic: 20,000 hits per day

Unlike the two previous unsigned artist sites, Musicunsigned doesn't attempt to be an online retailer and therefore doesn't sell CDs or downloads. Instead, it focuses on RealAudio streaming and acts as a forum at which A&R can preview unsigned artists' material, with the aim at this stage being to get a record deal for its artists rather than selling records – you have to walk before you can run. You'll have to pay to be on the site, but the upside is that you're competing with far fewer musicians. Your music also has to satisfy Musicunsigned's own A&R team before you're allowed on. Their successful track record includes the act Smokers Blend 3000, who secured a record deal with One Stop/Pinnacle after exposure on their site.

A&R Rating: ★★★

Popwire.com
Launched: May 1999
Software: QuickTime, Windows Media, RealAudio, MP3
Traffic: 15,000 hits per day

Popwire is a dedicated A&R site. It doesn't sell CDs but instead focuses all of its energy on securing deals for its acts. Popwire also offers the site's most listened-to artists a publishing deal as a step up to promoting them to record labels, although his should be resisted at all costs.

A&R Rating: ★★★

some tips before you sign up

You'll have to sign a short contract before any of the unsigned music web sites will allow you to join. Often, these contracts are actually displayed on the web site itself, and you'll have to scroll through and agreed to these before you can go any further. Some companies, such as Peoplesound, issue short contracts (in very small type) in their promotional leaflets. Try and make the effort to read the contract, no matter how boring it is, because you don't want to sign away any rights and then find that you can't get a deal with a "proper" record company. A few things to look for:

- The contract must be non-exclusive so that, if a label becomes interested in you, you can sign to them;

- You should be able to terminate the agreement whenever you want, simply by notifying the company. Usually, an e-mail to their web site should be sufficient;

- Any rights you grant to the company (ie to sell your CDs and to download and stream your music) should automatically cease when you terminate the contract;

- If the company is seeking a commission on income from any record deal you end up signing, limit this to a maximum of 20% on the first album advances only (exclusive of recording costs). They should only be able to receive a commission if you get the deal as a result of being discovered on their web site;

• At the moment, most sites are offering a royalty of 50% of net receipts to their artists, and this is the minimum that you should expect. MPReal.com are offering artists a 75% royalty of net receipts, and there is no reason why the others shouldn't match this figure.

how do labels view unsigned music web sites?

It has to be said that, at the moment, labels view unsigned music web sites with a fair degree of scepticism. Many A&R scouts have so far shown a distinct lack of enthusiasm for web site talent-spotting. The reasons for their reluctance to embrace the internet are: (a) quantity rather than quality is the watchword for too many web sites – it could take several hours of wading through unlistenable or just plain dull music to discover one gem; and (b) the record industry is dubious about the motives behind unsigned artist web sites. Note to unsigned music web sites: up the quality control! As one A&R scout at a major publisher recently put it, "Unless some barriers to entry are erected, we're still all going to be ankle-deep in dodgy demos."

There is even an argument that the very nature of unsigned music web sites will undermine what real A&R is all about by marginalising it. Do such sites ghettoise unsigned music by making young bands false promises? ("We'll get your music heard by thousands. We'll deliver you to the industry and the consumer. Just sign on the dotted line and join the several thousand other hopefuls jostling for attention.") Does the term "unsigned" give out negative connotations about the music that the sites are seeking to promote?

The A&R departments of record labels are also quick to point out that unsigned music web sites will come to nothing if they don't have true A&R talent – and this means not just discovering (or, in this case, simply hosting) new music; it's 99% about what you do after signing an act. Do Mudhut or Vitaminic have a proven track record in nurturing and developing raw talent? Do Peoplesound? (A Peoplesound executive, speaking at a conference I attended, spoke of being able to offer artists an alternative to the usual twelve-album deals. Hello! *Twelve* albums!) Are they making promises that they can't keep? How stringent are their A&R policies? Are these companies just chasing a big public share offering? There are still plenty of unanswered questions about the nature and likely success rate of these sites, so try and keep a rational perspective if you decide to take the plunge and put your music in their hands.

Although there is some justification for these criticisms, it's possible – if not probable – that one or two leading unsigned music web sites will soon emerge from the bunch, and these will be the ones with the most discriminating A&R policies and the best music. Indeed, there has already been at least one major-label internet signing, The Fighting Cocks (!), who were discovered by RCA's A&R director, Nick Raymonde, via a link to their own web site from the Band Register's web site.

the future for unsigned music web sites

Over the next couple of years, unsigned music web sites will come to play a more significant role for record industry talent scouts, and not just in helping them discover new acts. Web sites like Peoplesound and Vitaminic could revolutionise the way in which new bands are signed.

The music industry writes off $5 billion in unrecoverable investments each year because 95% of debut albums fail. The user data that Peoplesound and other sites generate could significantly improve this hit ratio, because A&R people will then have access to lots of useful information before a band is signed. For example, they will know of the artist's popularity in relation to their peer group and the demographics and location of their listeners.

Major labels may even use unsigned music web sites as feeders, in the same way that premier league football clubs have adopted local league sides in order to loan out their young players and monitor their progress. A band could similarly be signed on a development deal and test-marketed on, say, the Peoplesound web site. After a month or so on the site, the label will have a fairly clear idea about what kind and to how many people the band will appeal before they start investing in them heavily. In fact, Rob Dickins' new label, Instant Karma, did exactly this with their first signing, Helicopter Girl, whose debut single, 'Subliminal Punk', went to Number One on the Peoplesound Free Download chart. Dickins' label also developed a microsite for Helicopter Girl, which allowed fans to download the single and preview several tracks from the band's forthcoming album.

There's definitely a lot of potential in these ideas. In the meantime, unsigned music web sites will continue to offer young bands another area in which they can be discovered.

A final word of advice: make sure you choose the right web site to send your music to. You don't want your music to be buried under a morass of mediocrity, so sign up to a discerning site. Also, remember to keep sending tapes to the right people – A&R scouts will still frequent all of their usual haunts for the foreseeable future. Speaking of which…

live music showcases

Attending live gigs is a great way of finding out what a band is all about, and it always will be – that's one thing the internet isn't going to change. I remember being fortunate enough to catch The Stone Roses at Brixton in the last tour before Squire left, and after five years of having only the records to listen to it was an awe-inspiring experience to see them playing just a few feet away, tumbling onstage to the strains of 'I Wanna Be Adored'. A band may be discovered via an unsigned music web site, or from an internet-generated buzz, but A&R scouts will still want to see them perform live before committing to signing them. The continued success of the annual unsigned live music showcases, such as In The City, the New Music Seminar and South By Southwest, proves that playing live remains a key element of touting for a deal.

staying independent *with* a record deal

Okay, so it may be difficult to do without record companies in the early stages of your career, because of the sheer amount of money that labels are prepared to invest (and, to a lesser extent, because of their expertise). So, let's assume that record companies are going to retain their pre-eminence, at least in the short term. After all, it's likely that they'll continue to wield power, at least until the fall-out from major artists' renegotiating their contracts and releasing albums independently from their record companies filters down to ground level.

As a young band, your bargaining power is limited. Even so, the more you do for yourself before you even go anywhere near a record label, the stronger your position will be. You should be setting up your own web site and registering your domain name as soon as you know you've got something worth pursuing musically. If you get the music right (naturally this comes first, although some bands seem to forget this), and you have a professional attitude, everything should flow from this.

If you have access to good-quality recording equipment – preferably your own home studio – you'll be in a much stronger position. It's well worth seeking a little investment or financial help to purchase the right equipment, even a bank loan, to be self-sufficient from the outset. The less you give a record company to spend money on, the less you'll need them and the less likely you are to be dropped if the first album doesn't "shift units".

keeping control of your rights

Having got your web site up and running, registered your domain name and produced some excellent release-quality masters prior to contracting with the label, what next? Should your record company – and, for that matter, your publishing company – be able to acquire all rights in your recordings and compositions?

This is an important issue, perhaps *the* most important one that you'll face as you negotiate your record and publishing deals. Owning copyright has always been the surest way of making money in the music industry, and content is ever more valuable in the online marketplace. Where would AOL or any other service provider be with nothing to sell?

can labels have the right to offer your music for download?

Obviously, if the record company pays for the recordings they will own the copyright in the recordings – fair enough. But you need not necessarily allow one record company the right to exploit your music in all formats; there's no reason why you can't limit your grant of rights to ensure that the exploitation in a particular format, or by a particular method, is carried out by the company (not necessarily a *record* company) best able to undertake such exploitation. For example, why in effect sub-license digital rights to EMusic if the rights can be retained and licensed directly? Record companies will argue that they pay for the recording of artists' songs, but it is questionable whether this gives them the right to exploit those recordings in any format they choose.

Exploitation in different media requires expertise suitable to that particular medium. Theoretically, an ISP with broadband access and millions of subscribers worldwide should be better placed to get your music out there using the internet. Until record companies have a proven track record in online exploitation, they should be responsible only for sales through the usual retail channels.

split-territory deals

As the internet pushes back trading frontiers across the globe, another option is to seek split-territory deals to maximise income from the exploitation of recordings with the label best placed to promote you in a particular territory. For example, you may choose to sign to an independent in the UK who won't necessarily have a fully-formed digital distribution strategy outside the UK, if at all. In this case, you should limit their right to exploit downloads to the UK only and, as your profile rises, leave yourself open to sign a deal in North America, or even the world outside the UK, with Warner, for example, or with another company with a strong online presence.

your publishing rights

The internet is affecting not only record labels but also music publishing, as writers begin to question whether publishers should still acquire all rights to their work. One possible route is to examine a publisher's strengths in a particular media market. Some, for example, are very good at brokering *synch licences* – they enjoy good relations and/or have good contacts with broadcasters and can get the writer's music on film and TV. Others may concentrate on teaming up writers and producers, and so on.

Increasingly, the focus will be on exploiting copyrights in digital media, and you should limit the assignment of your rights to the media in which publishers are strong. Taking a lead from the TV and film industries, rights may become the subject of multiple layers of exploitation, with layers, or *windows*, specifically negotiated for individual media. If your publisher wishes to acquire digital rights, it should give an undertaking to exploit your songs digitally, or else lose that right.

Just as the importance of record companies will diminish as online exploitation starts to exceed sales of physical product, so ownership of copyright in compositions will take on even greater significance, and performance income may become a writer's main source of revenue. A lot depends on how successful the PRS, ASCAP and the other collection societies are in agreeing internet public performance charges and policing usage on the net. (Collection societies are covered in Chapter 12.)

If performance income does become the musician's biggest source of income (and it might, if pay-as-you-listen subscription, webcasting and streaming all take off), there may be no reason to sign a publishing deal at all. You can already register direct with the PRS, so why not bypass the publisher altogether? Let the agencies collect in the performance income and pay over the full 100%, less their (nominal) administration fee.

One of the main roles of a publisher is to administer and exploit catalogues as efficiently as possible. If a company specialising in collecting data is able to do that more cheaply and just as efficiently, publishers may find themselves cut out of the equation altogether. They, too, must justify their worth in the Internet Age.

internet releases – the way forward?

Black Crowes in not retro shock!

You may think it unlikely that you'll be able to restrict the rights that you grant to a label or publisher in this way, and at the moment you'd be right. However, as higher-profile acts start to put out records without following the normal record company route, the climate will change. This is happening already.

A year or so back, The Black Crowes hooked up with Led Zeppelin guitarist Jimmy Page and toured the States, playing a mix of Crowes/Zeppelin numbers to great acclaim. Nothing too unusual in that, you might say. Then they decided to document the tour by releasing a live album. Again, standard procedure (although live albums are notoriously poor sellers). What is unusual about this particular release is that The Black Crowes had recently fulfilled their recording commitment to the record label Def American and Jimmy Page was master of his own destiny for solo work. They wanted to put the record out straight away, on the back of the tour, but figured that it would take months to get it into the shops, taking the usual record company route. "Had we gone through a traditional major label marketing and distribution system," comments The Black Crowes' manager, Pete Angelus, "I think it's safe to say that it would have been four to six months before the record would have been in the stores."

So, who do you suppose put the record out? Not your traditional, run-of-the-mill record label, but Musicmaker.com, a dedicated internet record label. It was a groundbreaking release for the internet – the first internet-only album from a major act (or, in this case, two major acts).

Equally interesting was the way in which the album was marketed. Customers were given several options. They could:

• Order an 18-track CD with packaging and all the trimmings;

• Download any or all of the 19 tracks available from Musicmaker.com, paying per track downloaded;

• Choose five or more tracks to create their own custom CD version of the album. As Jimmy Page put it, "The listener becomes the A&R man. He's the one who chooses what tracks he wants on the album."

The wide range of choices available to the consumer highlights the internet's great flexibility in promoting a release. The one option most obviously missing from the above list, however, is a high street retail sale. To the disappointment of retailers across the globe, the album remained an internet-only release until July 2000, a good six months after appearing on the worldwide web, and even then major stores such as HMV refused to stock it after being snubbed on its initial release.

So, how did fans get to hear of its release? Via the internet – the Musicmaker.com site, the artists' own web sites (both official and unofficial) – and because Musicmaker serviced US radio with a one-track promo "single" and listeners were directed to their local radio station's web site for details on how to obtain the album.

The internet-release strategy certainly paid off. The album is the internet's biggest seller to date, and the promo single, 'What Is And What Should Never Be', became the first-ever internet-only single to make it into the Top 20 of *Billboard*'s mainstream rock chart.

Young, unknown artists are now putting their music out on the internet before they sign a record contract which prevents them from doing so. Major artists who have the ability to renegotiate their contracts or who have retained rights to download their music will soon follow suit. In turn, this will influence the way in which the music industry operates, and contracts at ground level for new artists will gradually come to reflect these changes.

For the immediate future, however, it will be only the established artists who really benefit. Remember the three reasons for the continued existence of record companies? They advance money to finance the cost of making records; they manufacture and market records; and they take away risk. Well, for a major artist – a Black Crowes, or a Jimmy Page – none of these apply, except possibly the label's willingness to underwrite the financial risk on a project. In the longer term, less well-known artists will increasingly be able to use the internet to engineer deals such as this one, and record companies will lose some of the power they have traditionally held over their artists' output.

It's interesting to speculate how different the outcome might have been in the Prince and George Michael label disputes if the internet had been as dominant ten years ago. My guess is that those artists would have used the net to help free them from their obligation to keep putting out records through one label, and to keep hold of some of their rights. Even if they had been unable to walk away, the net's potential for increased independence would have been obvious to them. George Michael was certainly very quick to embrace the internet with the formation of his internet-only record label, Aegean, in as early as 1997.

release music when you want, as you want

The internet will not only change the kinds of deals that artists strike with labels; it will also change the way in which artists release their music. Writing about Prince reminds me of one of the main problems that he had with Warner Bros – he was so prolific that they didn't want to keep putting out his records for fear of saturating the market. They also felt (with some justification) that quality control was inevitably going to take a back seat if Prince kept churning out albums in less time than it took to pronounce his subsequent "name". (Geffen never had this problem with The Stone Roses.)

If you're a member of Radiohead, you will already be familiar with the concept of sharing your personal struggles with the rest of the world, via your internet studio diary, as you recount the tortuous progress of your new album. It's a short step from this to bringing that diary to life by releasing snippets of outtakes, jams and works in progress to keep your fans updated and hungry for the final product. In fact, Radiohead weren't the only mega band to end the first year of the new millennium singing the praises of online promotion; following hot on their heels, U2 posted a track a week on their web site in the run-up to the release of their latest album, *All That You Can't Leave Behind*. The band also webcast the recording of the album exclusively on their site. Soon you will be able to release as much music as you want exactly when you want. Just finished putting down a free-form jazz exploration? Think your fans will "dig it"? Stick it out there on MP3 or another digital format.

Hard though it may be to imagine at the moment, the traditional ten- or eleven-track album format may eventually be supplanted by changing release patterns brought about by the internet. If artists feel like releasing tracks in bursts as and when they feel like it – two or three this month, maybe a whole "side" or suite a few months later – what's to stop them? Not the tastes of the record-buying public, if sales of the enduring *Now That's What I Call Music* compilation series are anything to go by. Mass audience tastes look set to push the new non-album format through. Music buyers – particularly the Woolworths/Asda variety – don't want to sit through a whole album by one act; if they buy an album, it's for the two or three hit singles, and they're the tracks that they'll program into the CD.

Changing listening habits are already making custom CDs a success, as stores such as Virgin's revamped V-Shop chain, Topshop and WH Smith will testify. Once the majors truly embrace the concept of giving the consumer what he wants and burn-your-own-compilation kiosks and booths start to become as common a feature in record stores as listening posts, custom CDs will really take off. In the meantime, though, watch out for your favourite artists announcing the release of their new single as an interactive CD-ROM exclusive, and their next album as a one-track-a-day download spread over two weeks, followed closely by the DVD release of the album featuring the edited webcam highlights of the band in the studio.

tales from the music business part I

relations with record labels – the Mainstream story

Once upon a time in the dim and distant past (well, not too distant), I was in a rock band signed to a fairly well known label – Nude Records, home to Suede and, er, Ultrasound. The band was called Mainstream. Heard of us? Well, probably not. Here's why…

We were signed in the summer of 1995, at a time when Britpop was at its height and hordes of A&R men traipsed from venue to venue (all somehow located in Camden Town) waving chequebooks at anyone sporting an Adidas sweatshirt and a Liam Gallagher attitude. As you can imagine, a lot of truly awful bands got signed. We weren't awful; we hated Britpop, and could see that it wasn't going to last, but nonetheless we were fortunate to be in the right place at the right time. We signed to Nude after only a handful of gigs and with an even smaller handful of songs, and were promptly thrown in a rehearsal room on a "lock-out" and told to come out four months later with an "identity" and some material.

This was otherwise known as a *development deal*. Unfortunately, the only developing we did was developing the ability to go out in the evening, spending our copious advances, showing up for rehearsals at two in the afternoon and packing up at four after inspiration mysteriously failed to show up with us. Actually, we did work quite hard at times, but cabin fever became a bit of a problem and we didn't progress as much as we or the label would have liked. All of a sudden, the development deal was over. Things seemed to be moving incredibly fast around us. The pressure was soon on, as Nude exercised their option to record an album, and we set about writing and trying to gain live and press exposure.

The upshot of this was that we did our developing as a band in public (insofar as journalists saw our earliest gigs and heard our earliest demos) and in a pressured environment, where mistakes could prove very expensive. Our first two singles were scrapped at a cost of some £10,000 after flaws in the writing and performing departments were exposed by a seasoned producer.

On our first tours, we gradually ironed out these flaws and settled on a musical direction not entirely to Nude's liking and generally out of kilter with the prevailing pop vibe. The label sensed that we wanted to be a rock band, took a wild punt and hired Billy Duffy (former axe hero with '80s rock monoliths The Cult) to produce our album. Billy hadn't produced before but, having blown the previous session, we felt that we should agree.

As bands often do, we developed a siege mentality, blaming the PR people for not getting enough press, the plugger for not getting us on daytime radio and the label for not pushing the band hard enough. In truth, the writing direction became increasingly confused as advice was proffered, if not always sought, from all corners. The end result was an album recorded piecemeal, at vast expense and in several different studios (including the legendary Rockfield, Mickie Most's RAK and Monnow Valley) using several different engineers and with more than a passing nod in the direction of our (actually pretty eclectic) record collections. It was very good in places – check out 'Castaway' and the Hammond/flute jam on 'Transatlantic' – but by the time we'd finished it, it was the summer of 1998 and our time had well and truly come and gone. All that we and Nude had to show for some quarter of a million pounds of investment, alas, was the odd Radio 1 playlist and an occasional appearance on *The Chart Show*. On the day of release, huge quantities of Mainstream albums were conspicuous by their absence in record racks the length and breadth of the country.

I think that the album eventually sold something like 2,000 copies in the UK, although it fared a little better abroad. I remember thinking a week or so after it had been released that we could have put this album out two years before, as soon as we'd accumulated ten (not as good) songs, having spent a tenth of the money, and it would have done just as well, probably a lot better.

So, in the words of the press photographer who gatecrashed George Best's luxury hotel suite in London's Hilton and found the Manchester United star resplendent and sipping champagne surrounded by a bevy of beautiful girls, where did it all go wrong, George? In short, the moral of the story is to get your act together and pursue as clear a vision as possible before you sign a record deal. When you're signed to the label, it's important to preserve as much of your independence as you can. Retain as much creative and financial control as possible. Relations with your label are important. Creatively, they need to understand where you're coming from in order to market you and plan the best way of breaking your music into an over-populated marketplace. This area, in particular, is where the internet is going to be a real benefit to artists, as it allows them to communicate with their fans directly, sell and promote merchandise and exclusive tracks, monitor and target audience reaction in the run-up to release dates, announce tour dates and so on.

It's also very important to see the bigger picture and get your records out when the opportunity presents itself. The internet should help you get your music out quicker and more fluidly – you'll be able to use it as a testing ground, so you won't have to agonise over whether to release something or not. So often bands obsess over trivialities – an edit in a video they don't like, or the wrong design for an advert. Worse still, they argue endlessly over things like the middle eight in a song that is inherently mediocre. Forget it. Go write something better and then put it out.

The Mainstream story probably reflects the experiences of many other bands signed around the same period – often for silly amounts of money – who struggled to deliver the goods, went deep into the red and were dropped by the label one album into their careers. For the record label, there's always next year's big thing; for the musician, though, the chance probably won't come around again. It's a salutary lesson for artists and record companies alike.

chapter 6

artists vs record companies

T *he music business is a cruel and shallow money trench, a long plastic hallway where thieves and pimps run free, and good men die like dogs... There's also a negative side..."*
– Hunter S Thompson

new rules for record companies and artists?

The internet is forcing record companies and artists to re-evaluate both their creative and contractual relationships. The areas of potential conflict in negotiations and renegotiations are numerous, and they can be of potentially damaging consequence. A great deal hinges – legally, at least – on the wording of the document that governs those relationships: the recording agreement itself. At this point in time, the template for this new interaction between artist and label is being thrashed out in the boardrooms of law offices in Los Angeles, New York and London. Labels and artists are now being forced to analyse key aspects of their contractual relationship afresh. Inevitably, the focus is on royalty rates, granting of rights, ownership of web sites, term and product commitment.

the pre-internet position – what do existing contracts say?

Existing record contracts – those drafted in the heady days of industrial-strength vinyl, gatefold sleeves, gigs on the university circuit and one-album-a-year cycles – put the balance of power firmly with the label. In all probability, existing contracts say very little of direct relevance to the internet, although in most cases the original wording can be interpreted to encompass the arrival of online media and the electronic distribution of music. There are two main areas of the contract that need close examination: rights granted and royalties.

rights granted

Record companies have always either owned copyrights in artists' master recordings outright from the time of their inception or have sought to secure as wide-ranging a licence of rights as possible, often by using a catch-all phrase to cover exploitation "by any means devised or to be devised". Sometimes, the record company will be clearly restricted to selling only physical product. In the main, though, record companies should have the right to sell recordings by whatever means they wish, and even if they don't then their ownership of copyright in the master recordings will enable them to prevent anyone else from doing so. This being the case, it must then be determined whether it can be clearly discerned from the contract how much the artist should receive from internet exploitation of his recording.

royalties

The major concern for the record company is that, in the absence of any expressly stated provision to the contrary, the artist will claim that the proceeds arising from digital distribution fall within the category of the label's ancillary/flat-fee income, and will therefore (usually) entitle him to a royalty of 50% of the record company's net receipts. This will substantially eat into the record company's margin and, given that new media and other record-configuration clauses have traditionally been drafted to cover only physical product (ie DAT or MiniDisc), will leave the label with nowhere to turn. The only way forward in this situation is to renegotiate the royalty provisions.

negotiation

An established artist's renegotiating position is strong because the internet means that, these days, artists don't need their record companies as much. Meanwhile, major artists with only one or two albums left to deliver won't be quick to agree to new, less favourable royalty provisions. For new artists, particularly those courted by more than one label, the chances of resisting the record company's demands in this area aren't as bad as one might think. The internet has caught record companies unaware, and a coherent online strategy, as far as contracting with artists is concerned, has so far been conspicuous by its absence. In other words, the majors haven't got their stories straight yet!

the record contract

remake/remodel

The internet is changing the way in which record companies exploit their recordings and the way in which artists think about releasing their material. Traditional album formats may well give way to more regular releases of new material in shorter, three- or four-track bursts. Indeed, labels won't always be dealing with straight recording contracts in their relationships with artists; the emphasis has shifted – partly through the influence of the quick-turnaround dance/garage scene in the UK – to the release of singles and short-term projects, with musicians working for several different acts and producers. Today, short one- or two-track licensing agreements and "featured artist" agreements are common currency in the record industry. Fluidity is the key.

As a consequence of this, the three-year album cycle peddled by the major artists will almost certainly disappear. When a song can travel from a home recording studio to the form of a finished, digital master to a first public airing on the internet in the space of time it takes for Ocean Colour Scene to master a Small Faces riff, it will be harder to sustain such lengthy gaps between releases. Prince will have a field day!

Labels must be alive to these new trends in their full-scale recording contracts. As well as being aware of how these trends impact on product commitment (a subject covered later), they must ensure that they're totally covered in terms of being able to release anything in any shape or form, as technology and market tastes dictate.

Let's look at the major areas in a typical record contract in turn and examine how the internet is going to change things for both labels and artists.

grant of rights and compilations

Exploitation through compilations – both compiling and recompiling material – will become a major source of revenue. Does the label have an unencumbered right to license to third-party compilations or is it limited to *Now*-style compilation albums? When does a compilation become a resequencing? What royalty will be paid on third-party compilations? These are all issues that will need to be addressed.

The Argument

Label – The record company will want to ensure that it is granted not only the right to digitally download but also the right to resequence and recompile master recordings and, in addition, the right to download individual master recordings in any combination and at any price considered appropriate without infringing the artist's creative approval.

Artist – Contracts have traditionally allowed artists either consultation rights or, more often, outright control over creative (as opposed to commercial) issues. For example, resequencing the running order of an album could compromise the integrity of the record as an artistic statement, as a great deal of careful thought and planning goes into programming the selection of tracks, taking into consideration tempo, key, cross-fades, segues and so on. Similarly, recompiling masters for, say, "greatest hits" albums is usually limited by artists' lawyers to no more than once during the term of the agreement, and then once after the term has expired (if the artist is recouped).

Direct downloading and custom CDs both attack the artistic integrity of an album. If a consumer chooses to download his or her favourite four tracks from an album, the record company are effectively allowing its resequencing. This should always be subject to the artist's approval in the usual way.

Label – A compromise position has to be reached. While respecting the artist's need to retain overall creative control, the commercial reality of custom CDs and subscription-based or other on-demand services is too great an opportunity for either the label or the artist to miss out on. If the traditional ten-track, 45-minute album gradually becomes an outmoded way of releasing material, it will be imperative for both parties to be well placed to take advantage of new streams of income. Seeking the artist's approval every time somebody wants to include the artist's work on a custom CD would be impractical, and so, as a middle ground, the artist's approval should be sought only if more than two tracks from any one album are to be licensed for compilation usage on the same CD. The right to automatically license two or less tracks would be granted to the label.

In addition, the label may argue that, as it's the consumer and not the label who is doing the compiling with custom CDs, any restriction preventing the *record company* from coupling the artist's masters wouldn't apply to custom CDs. However, it may be hard to justify that this approach is within the spirit of the agreement. Still, it's really up to artists' representatives to obtain clarification on this point.

Artist – The right to compile may be agreed, but what about royalties? Normally, record companies pay a reduced royalty rate, frequently at half the normal rate, and this is in addition to a pro-rata reduction in the royalty as a result of having, say, only one out of the ten tracks on the compilation. Therefore, if the artist's royalty was 20% of the dealer price and the compilation wholesaled at £10, a half-rate royalty would be 10% of £10 divided by ten (pro-rationing), equalling 10p. If custom CD compilations and digitally downloaded compilations become standard formats, the artist should argue strongly against receiving a half-rate royalty.

The record companies can't have it both ways. If labels wish to take advantage of new trends in market tastes – in particular custom CD compilations – then they must be prepared to pay a front-line royalty for a front-line form of exploitation. A half-rate royalty is unjustifiable.

royalties on hybrid sales

Royalties from records sold via the internet will differ depending on how those records are distributed. Exploitation will be either (a) through *hybrid sales* (in other words, records and CDs etc being delivered by mail order as normal physical product, as a result of orders placed via the internet) or (b) through records sold by means of direct download to the end-user's hard drive, with both order and delivery carried out online.

The Argument

Artist – There are two ways to approach the issue of mail order sales fulfilled via the internet. First, artists should argue that, as the label's distribution costs are limited to postage and packaging charges and limited fulfilment, rather than the usual distribution fee, the label is enjoying an increased profit margin on such sales, and that the artist should therefore participate in that increase.

Label – The label will counter-argue that it is having to underwrite the cost of operating two different forms of distribution (at least in the short term): one for e-commerce sales by mail order and digital delivery and the other for the traditional method of distribution, from warehouse to distributor to high street retailer. Until one truly supplants the other, the increased profit margin from hybrid sales will be needed to justify and fund both operations.

Artist – If this avenue proves fruitless, the artist should try and get the label to agree that hybrid sales of records will, in any event, mirror the provisions in the record contract with regard to normal retail/wholesale record sales, so that the label doesn't make any negative special allowances for hybrid sales. For example, such sales should not be treated as standard one-off mail order sales, thereby attracting a half-rate royalty. Alternatively, if the label does impose some form of penalty on hybrid sales, the artist should seek to obtain a provision preventing the label from applying a further reduction for records sold via the internet at mid or budget price.

Firstly, if the label is selling to an affiliated joint venture (such as BMG selling to Getmusic), the artist should ensure that the label isn't entitled to sell to its affiliate at less than the full dealer price for a conventional retail sale.

royalties on digital downloads

The formula for calculating an artist's royalty rate on digital downloads could go several ways, but more likely than not it will end up as one more complicated variation on the headline royalty rate stated in the artist's contract. Taking a positive view, the task of having to incorporate digital downloads, streaming income and so on into traditional royalty clauses should provide labels and their business affairs teams with a great opportunity to revisit the drafting of these clauses from scratch. After all, very few artists (or lawyers!) understand them.

Record labels should jettison their time-honoured attitude of making the royalty provisions in a record contract the most laborious and labyrinthine read imaginable and should instead concentrate on making the royalty provisions easy to follow. (The saving on legal fees would be justification in itself!) Then, artists would have a clear understanding of what they would earn from sales of their records.

Barriers to change remain, however. Record companies like to make the headline royalty rate appear as high as possible – it's an attractive way of selling the deal to the artist. However, no matter how impressive 20% of dealer price appears at first glance, once the artist's lawyer has painstakingly explained that, after deducting packaging costs and special packaging costs for gatefold sleeves featuring cardboard cut-outs of the band, an allowance for real free goods and special free goods, a half-rate royalty for record-club sales, a three-quarter-rate royalty for sales at mid price, a half-rate royalty for records sold on the backs of cereal packets and a reduced rate on all sales to the artist's grandmother in the first six weeks after initial release in the minor territories, the artist's initial enthusiasm will tend to wane somewhat.

Okay, I'm exaggerating a tad, and in fact several of the royalty deductions are valid intrusions into the headline rate. Nonetheless, some deductions could easily be absorbed into the label's royalty formula before arriving at the royalty base price without altering its profit margin, simply by allowing for the recalculation and lowering the headline royalty accordingly. For example, once everyone gets used to the fact that 20% of dealer price with packaging deductions is more or less the same thing as 16% of dealer price with no packaging deductions, 16% will soon be seen as the norm for a fair-to-middling benchmark rate.

If this approach is taken universally for all sales of records in any configuration and by any means or method of distribution, it will be relatively easy to assimilate into new contracts the potentially complicated area of sales by digital download.

setting the royalty rate across the board

The key is to set the royalty rate by reference to a fixed amount of pounds or dollars per unit, based on a given sale price. The royalty would then increase or decrease on a sliding scale, and the value wouldn't depend on the format sold or the method of distribution. The only variable would be the actual sale price of each unit sold.

In licensing deals with US labels, it's common for UK record companies to ask for what is known as a "dollars-and-cents" royalty rate. The royalty provisions of US labels tend to be even more complicated than those used by their UK counterparts (and US lawyers tend to be very intransigent when it comes to negotiating them), so by asking for a specific royalty of, say, $1.50 per sale, the licensor label no longer has to be concerned about whether or not packaging, club sales etc are incorporated into the royalty calculation, because they are guaranteed $1.50 regardless. It also makes a lot of the small print redundant.

There's no reason why this method shouldn't also govern contracts between labels and artists. Currently, many new-release CDs retail at around £14 (although online retail pressures are forcing this price down). If this figure is used by way of illustration, the artist's royalty can be set at £1.60, for example, with no packaging deduction. If the actual sales price is £12, the royalty would decrease commensurately to £1.37, and if the album sold for £16, the royalty would increase to £1.83.

Mid-price and budget-price sales can still be built into the equation simply by multiplying the price achieved by a percentage, such as, say, 75% for mid-price sales and 50% for budget sales. This approach will still permit a percentage of records manufactured to be given away to radio stations for promotional purposes and so on.

Although this approach to the calculation of royalties will initially appear to be a radical and time-consuming process to record companies (after all, it would mean that they would have to conduct a comprehensive review of internal profit-and-cost structures in order to determine the level at which to set the royalty rate on any given retail price), in the end it makes as much sense for labels as it does for artists. A chief source of man-hours and aggravation for any label (particularly independent companies with small complements of accounting staff) is preparing bi-annual royalty statements and running software programs with complex parameters built in to allow for packaging, mid-price sales and other exceptions. The simpler the method of calculation, the easier the preparation of royalty statements.

For sales by way of digital download, the royalty clause would simply state that the artist's royalty rate would be calculated on the increased or decreased royalty base price. If the label's fulfilment provider pays the label, say, £6.50 after the deduction of credit-card transaction fees and its fulfilment charges, the artist would receive a royalty of 74p.

The Argument

Artist – Most artists appreciate that record companies are taking a risk with regard to e-commerce, but it would appear that some labels are suggesting that the artist should underwrite this risk. These labels are arguing that, if their receipts from digital downloads are less than the dealer price for a conventional physical sale, the royalty rate should be reduced to half rate. Some labels are also suggesting that artists should suffer a royalty break in order to take into consideration the costs of research and development. This may have been justifiable in the early days of CD manufacture, but surely not in the online marketplace.

Label – Record companies will want the artist to be entitled to the otherwise applicable royalty rate, calculated on the applicable price, depending on the configuration sold (ie album or single), providing that the label's receipts in respect of these sales are more than, say, 75% of the label's or its licensees' dealer price for sales of records at full price. If that figure falls below 75% then the artist's royalty should be only half of the otherwise applicable rate.

Even though the record company will probably have to agree to review its internet royalty provisions in good faith following the second or third anniversary of the contract, it will seek to ensure that it isn't obliged to increase the royalty rate as a result of such a review.

public performance fees

A point worth noting concerning fees arising as a result of the public performance of recordings is the issue of the artist's entitlement to the PPL (Phonographic Performance Limited) income from online exploitation. Ordinarily, there's no need to expressly state in the record contract that artists should receive a percentage of PPL income because, following the Copyright And Related Rights Regulations of 1996, artists are automatically entitled to receive 50% of PPL income direct from the PPL (provided that they're registered). However, as we'll see in Chapter 12, the PPL aren't currently authorised to grant blanket licences on behalf of their members for the online exploitation of recordings. This means that online music users will have to negotiate directly with the record companies themselves. In such a situation, you can be sure that the fee negotiated by the label will pass straight to the label itself, unless there is an express provision to the contrary written into the record contract. Artists' lawyers should therefore anticipate the possibility that the label will *source license*, thus circumventing the collecting societies, and ask for 50% of the label's receipts in such an event.

packaging deductions

Sales of digital downloads represent a great opportunity to finally do away, once and for all, with an artificial means of lowering artists' royalties. If the record has no physical form, how can the label justify charging for its packaging?

The Argument

Label – Record labels will seek to incorporate standard packaging deductions into the royalty calculation for digital downloads on the basis that they are an acceptable element of the royalty calculation provision in the recording agreement. Labels will also argue that the packaging will continue to have value to consumers that download material, because the consumer will either be downloading the artwork itself or viewing the artwork on a web site, and the content of such artwork will be affecting their choice of whether or not to buy.

Artist – Artists should ignore such spurious reasoning. The record industry knows that the percentages that it charges for packaging costs are a fabrication and do not, in fact, reflect the real cost of packaging. A product with no physical form doesn't warrant a physical packaging charge.

web site ownership

This is one of the major areas of debate in the current drafting of record contracts. The ownership of artists' web sites has been a source of controversy ever since Sony brought the issue out into the open halfway through 1999, when they declared that their standard recording contracts would contain a clause giving it ownership and/or control of its artists' web sites. Can Sony justify such a stance? Is this a route that other record companies should be pursuing? At the time of writing, Universal have already followed Sony's lead, and other majors look set to follow suit.

Negotiation will focus mainly on who owns what. From an artist's perspective, the web site would ideally be funded and owned by him. There would be a hypertext link to the label's own web site, and the label would provide a licence – free of charge – for the use of up to, say, 60 seconds of the artists' recordings for promotional purposes.

Increasingly, labels will try and insist on ownership of the site itself. If the artist has already registered a site in his or her name and refuses to transfer ownership, or is unwilling to contemplate label ownership in any circumstances, the label will seek to obtain (at the very least!) an exclusive, perpetual and irrevocable licence to use the registered web site name.

There's no reason why an artist shouldn't be amenable to the label setting up an "artist presence" owned by the artist. The artist can even grant the label an exclusive licence to use the URL for the sole purpose of selling records during the course of the term of the contract. However, the artist shouldn't agree that this will be his sole and exclusive music presence on the internet, as clearly there may be other authorised third-party sites. For example, the artist's publisher may wish to set up a web site.

The Argument

Label – Ostensibly, Sony's main justification for seeking ownership of their artists' web sites is to ensure that their artists don't sell records direct to their fans, either by download or mail order. Given the amount of money invested in making an artist successful, particularly in marketing their image and recordings, Sony's attitude appears to be understandable.

Artist – This argument is easily countered. Selling records would contravene the artist's warranties in their record contract, and they aren't going to do it without clearing it first and agreeing to split the income with the label. In 1999, Jamiroquai successfully argued that their site was not going to be used solely for the sale of records, and that therefore the proprietary rights to the site belonged to the band. Sony were forced to climb down on this occasion, but the act in question was one with significant bargaining power, and not all acts will be so successful.

In fact, the real reason why labels seek ownership of their artists' web sites is because they want to make sure that they take their slice of potentially lucrative new revenue streams which might otherwise pass directly to the artists. Heaven forbid! These new areas of income – in particular, the selling of merchandise and, in the near future, concert tickets – are potentially of as much significance as the revenue derived from the digital distribution of records. Record companies are worried that the sale of these products over the internet isn't covered by their artists' recording contracts, unlike the sale of records.

Label – Record labels, however, may feel justifiably uneasy about handing over so much control to their artists. They feel that retailers, merchandisers and concert promoters already have too much power in the areas of pricing and stocking, and don't want to relinquish similar power to artists. Moreover, labels won't want to be prevented from obtaining direct access to important marketing information, such as web visitors' e-mail and/or home addresses. In any event, the label certainly won't allow the artist to sell records from its web site, as this will cut across the label's exclusivity, which it has spent considerable sums of money obtaining.

Artist – Selling records from an artist's site is difficult to justify, but if a proper revenue split is calculated it would be foolish to turn down potential sales simply because the customer came to the artist's web site first. (After all, how many ordinary music fans know the name of their favourite artist's record label?) It may be that the sale of records from or via the artist's web site may be justified by the inclusion of a link to the label's home page and a bounty, or referral fee, paid to the artist for introducing the sale. The record company would then retain control of fulfilling the customer's order – which, in any case, it is better placed to do.

If a label insists on owning the artist's web site – thereby guaranteeing itself a piece of the action – instead of allowing the artist to control his own media channels and to access consumers directly, then the following safeguards should be inserted into the contract to protect the artist's position.

- Ask for extra consideration – perhaps an additional advance recoupable solely from ancillary web site income. After all, the label wouldn't have asked for these rights 18 months ago, so where is the consideration now? (A bit of a try-on, admittedly.)

- Watch out for the key area of subscription where consumers pay a monthly fee to the label/service provider, which then enables them to either stream or download all of the tracks licensed by the subscription service in unlimited quantities – in the case of Time Warner and EMI mergers, no doubt via AOL. Does the contract allow the label to exploit masters as they please and in any configuration? As we saw earlier, approvals and control for the artist are the key; the label shouldn't be permitted to download more than, say, two or three masters and/or make them available for subscription without the artist's consent.

- Any costs incurred by the label in setting up and maintaining the web site should be non-recoupable or, at worst, only recoupable from ancillary web site income, with possibly the first, say, £20,000 being non-recoupable. Alternatively, if the label is only incurring internal overhead costs (which is unlikely), these would not be recoupable at all. If the label goes out of house to a third-party web site design specialist, the costs involved would then be recoupable to a maximum of 50% only. In such a situation, as the artist will be involved in the development of the web site, he would effectively have joint control over the budget.

- Ensure that the artist has control over banners, advertisements and links on the web site. Some of these links may even be to the label's other artist web sites!

- Ensure that all ancillary income derived from the web site (including bounties, or referral fees) is not cross-collateralised with advances and other recoupable costs paid to the artist arising from the main body of the recording agreement. Such web site income should be split 75/25 or 80/20 in the artist's favour. At the very least, the artist should have favoured-nations protection here.

- Creative approval should be required both during and after the term over the content of any home page created for the artist by the label.

The argument about the ownership of the web site is a difficult one, but given that artists have traditionally kept hold of their merchandising rights in record contracts, and that live concert promotion isn't the domain of a company specialising in funding and marketing recordings, it may be hard for labels to justify claiming ownership or control of artists' web sites. The balance of bargaining power, however, is against a young, unsigned act (unless they are the focus of a bidding war), so it is likely that, in time, it will become an accepted practice for the ownership of an artist's web site to be licensed – at least for the duration of the contract – to the record label.

webcasts and other digital broadcasts

With the convergence of delivery technologies, webcasts and other live broadcasts of concert performances via digital media will become increasingly common. Although NetAid wasn't a success financially (or artistically – what a line-up!), and was prey to numerous technical hitches, it nevertheless illustrated the potential audience impact that simultaneous streamed performances can have, in global terms.

So, what role will record companies have in supervising or participating in the income from this new concert arena? A fairly significant one, if labels have their say.

The Argument

Label – The label will argue that a proposed digital-quality distribution of new material recorded and paid for by the record company gives it every right to seek to limit the artist's ability to webcast such performances. In addition, the label will argue that it has a legitimate interest in a number of aspects of any proposed live concert broadcast by the artist. In particular, the label will want approval over:

- Any media through which it is proposed to exploit the concert;

- Any more than one such concert taking place in each of the UK and the US during any one contract period;

- Any record or video releases of the concert;

- Transmission dates, in order to avoid conflicts with the label's marketing plans;

- Content, particularly if the proposed event will substantially involve the performance of new material.

Artist – Webcasts of live performances are of immense benefit to the artist as a potential source of revenue and as a valuable promotional tool. In the first instance, artists should seek to exclude cybergigs and unedited live performances from the grant of rights to the label altogether. The artist can safely agree on a right of consultation with the label regarding the media of exploitation. With regard to limiting the number of concerts, both label and artist have a vested interest in avoiding overkill, but the artist should seek a maximum of broadcasting, say, three live cybergigs per year.

Label – Record or video releases of the concert are clearly the domain of the label, which should have final approval. The label should also have a right of approval over the proposed transmission dates for such concerts, but only if they are scheduled for three months either side of any album release. The same goes for the inclusion of new material – if the album has been in the shops for six months, it's not really new any more, and if the gig is aired shortly before the release of an album, it will serve as a taster.

Artist – One final bone of contention will be whether the label is able to participate in revenues derived from cybergigs. Traditionally, labels haven't derived any income from live concerts, and this shouldn't really change just because the gig is broadcast over the internet. Provided that the label has approved those aspects in which it has a say, there can be no justification for it seeking a share of its artists' revenues.

term and territory

Issues regarding territory aren't so much about labels and artist as about conflict between labels and other labels. Split-territory deals were covered in the previous chapter, although this isn't likely to be an option for a young band signing their first contract, unless they are being courted by several labels. However, in years to come, alliances with technology and service providers will form part of a band's armoury, and record labels will be earmarked to fulfil only specific functions in those specific territories in which they have a track record.

For now, though, split-territory deals are more common where the artist has had some success and is licensing to two or more labels. (Usually, USA/Canada is the domain of one label, while the other takes the rest of the world.) In the past, this arrangement hasn't caused too many problems, although clauses dealing with simultaneous releases and the mutual funding of promo videos and remixes etc have had to be inserted into deals of this nature.

Of course, the internet changes all of this. Both record labels are likely to want to own the right to digitally upload and stream the artist's music. Also, both will probably wish to host an official web site. Moreover, numerous online retailers will be legitimately selling CDs by mail order over the net, taking customer orders from around the world. The internet's worldwide accessibility could lead to each label poaching customers from the other.

There is a very real danger that a consumer in the UK could buy the CD from the artist's official US web site, where it is being sold for £2-£3 cheaper. There are really only two ways around this. One is for the labels to agree not to sell or allow downloads outside their respective territories. (This is logistically possible in the case of downloads, as the e-mail addresses and credit-card billing details of their customers should alert the labels to the customer's location.) The other option is to accept that consumer power will win out and allow the selling out of territory to take place – with a percentage of the out-of-territory revenue going to the label which territorially had the right to make the sale.

The length, or *term*, of the deal is unlikely to be altered significantly by the internet, although the way in which it is calculated may well change. At present, the term is defined by reference to an artist's recording commitment, usually in cycles of one album per option. As artists' recording and release patterns evolve, this will no longer necessarily make sense, and record deals may start to resemble publishing agreements in that they define a contract period by reference to a certain number of recordings delivered (or released, in this case). It will be interesting to see how this develops as internet releases become more commonplace.

One aspect worth noting in relation to the artist's ability to terminate the term of the agreement early (in specified territories, at least) is the foreign-release commitment given by the record label. Ordinarily, if the label agrees to, say, release the artist's latest album within 90-120 days of its UK release in the "major territories" (usually the USA, Japan, Australia, Canada, France, Germany and, possibly, Benelux), then the artist is able either to get the rights back for the territory in which the album remains unreleased or, occasionally, to get *all* rights back (ie including future albums) for that territory.

The internet, of course, rather complicates matters. Many labels are now trying to argue that, by making the album available for download, they are discharging their obligation to release in overseas territories, on the basis that the internet is a worldwide medium.

This should be resisted at all costs. The artist should specify that the release commitment means the actual release of physical copies of the album – sales through normal retail channels via bricks-and-mortar record stores.

accounting and reporting sales

Accounting and reporting sales figures can cause great tension between artists and labels. Royalty statements invariably seem to be delivered late, are difficult to follow and contain numerous inaccuracies. (It's funny how these mistakes never seem to be in the artist's favour!) For those artists who suspect that they have been seriously under-accounted to, they should hire a firm of accountants to audit the record company's books. Be warned, however, that this is a time-consuming and very expensive business. It may also irreparably damage relations with the label, and should only be attempted if the artist has had a considerable amount of success. Otherwise, the cost is prohibitive.

The biggest problem that artists come up against when conducting an audit is not being able to access manufacturing records. If the label says that they've sold 20,000 records in the UK, and you know that they manufactured 50,000, there should be 30,000 records gathering dust in a warehouse near Swindon – it's easy to pinpoint the inaccuracies. Similarly, the artist should have access to (extracts from) statements from third-party licencees in order to be able to accurately check overseas sales figures.

Traditionally, it's been very hard for artists to obtain access to either manufacturing records or licencees' statements. Now, though, the internet should improve artists' abilities to view their sales figures both more regularly and with more assurance as to their accuracy. All sales arising from online exploitation – both hybrid sales and downloads – should be automatically logged and stored as electronic data, and this data should be transparently available to all artists accessing a secured web site. Theoretically, this online account report should update automatically whenever a sale or download is processed on the system. In this way, an artist will always be kept abreast of sales. However, just to be on the safe side, the artist should make sure that his audit rights entitle him to access the electronic log information.

moral rights

Introduced to the UK by the 1988 Copyright, Designs And Patents Act, moral rights are a relatively recent creation which allow an artist to assert ownership of a composition and to object to its derogatory treatment. For instance, Noel Gallagher successfully prevented The Smurfs from releasing a cover version of 'Wonderwall' by asserting that such a rendition would be derogatory of the original. It has become commonplace for labels and publishers to obtain waivers of moral rights in their contracts, as this means that their artists, as authors, cannot assert their moral rights, although they still retain ownership of them. (It's impossible to assign moral rights.) However, this is a sensitive issue for artists, and one which takes on greater significance in the digital environment.

Artists should ensure that, if they're forced to waive their moral rights in the contract, they obtain an exemption in respect of online distribution, or at least some form of protection to help them deal with a situation where their music is digitally manipulated or altered by either their label or a third party.

artists' negotiation checklist

This chapter has covered a lot of ground, and not all of it is straightforward, so here's a quick run through the key issues to look for in a record contract concerning the internet, if you're either the artist or representing the artist.

- Ensure that physical sales of CDs by online record stores via the internet aren't treated as falling within the definition of "club sales" – they shouldn't attract a half-rate royalty.

- If a record company is proposing to enter into a label deal with a digital distribution company for its catalogue, request that a pro-rata share of the advance it receives from the third party should be paid directly to the artist.

- Ensure that the artist receives the full 100% album royalty rate for digital downloads, rather than the single rate or a "new format" rate, if the royalty is calculated on dealer price or its retail equivalent.

- In the event that the royalty is expressed as a percentage of the label's net receipts, look to obtain at least 50% of the net profit and ensure that permitted expenses deducted off the top are limited to those incurred and actually paid by the label. Check what is being deducted. Ask for evidence of the fulfilment provider's charges if the artist is being asked to bear half of them.

- Ensure that downloads to customers outside the UK are paid at the full UK royalty rate, and that these payments won't suffer territorial deductions. There are no boundaries on the internet, and therefore no justification for requesting deductions in different jurisdictions.

- If the artist cannot obtain the above, confirm that the territorial royalty rate that is applied will be the rate for the country in which the order is sourced. (This is likely to be either the UK or the USA.)

- Ensure that the artist suffers no packaging deductions on digital downloads.

- Ensure that the artist has approval over the distribution of singles downloaded for free as promotional devices for albums.

- Ensure that the artist has the right of approval over the choice of material to be released to consumers for custom-burned CD albums.

- Free promotional downloads shouldn't be used to promote sales of records by the label's other artists.

- Ensure that a full-rate royalty is paid on tracks licensed to compilation albums, custom CDs and so on.

- There should be a good-faith review of the label's royalty provisions on a regular basis for both hybrid sales and for those undertaken by way of online delivery.

a word about publishing

Throughout this chapter, references have been made to the way in which the internet is affecting record contracts. However, it isn't just the relationship between the artist and the record label that's under the microscope; relations between writers and their publishers are also evolving, and publishing contracts are now reflecting this.

Publishing is a less controversial area – publishers don't pay for recordings, and these days they don't shape an artist's career in the way that they did in the '50s and '60s. Then, in the Tin Pan Alley era of inhouse writing teams for artists who didn't write their own material, publishers controlled all of the major writers and could choose those to whom they licensed songs. Artists and their labels were at the publishers' mercy. However, Lennon and McCartney and Bob Dylan threw that particular rulebook out of the window.

Nowadays, publishing is seen as a valuable commodity. Publishers are like banks – they administer and process the collection of money from around the world, usually via a network of sub-publishers or via their overseas offices. The truth is that writers need publishers a lot less than they need record companies, particularly when they become successful.

The internet will mean that writers need publishers even less. As we touched on in the previous chapter, performance income may become writers' main source of revenue. Writers already register directly with the PRS (or the BMI/ASCAP in the States), and by law they are entitled to receive half of all income derived from public performance direct (ie the *writer's* share). In addition, publishers usually pass on half of their share (ie the *publisher's* share) to the writer under the terms of their contract. If writers bypassed their publishers altogether, they would lose out on a third of their public performance revenue.

The good news for writers is that performing rights and mechanical rights collecting societies around the world are becoming increasingly streamlined. In the UK, the PRS and the MCPS have forged the Music Alliance, and are now able to link up digitally with many of their overseas counterparts. If writers are able to register with both and allow both to collect revenue on their behalf, they will suffer only the collecting societies' administration fee (around 5%). This compares favourably with a publisher's standard commission of 25%.

The online revolution should really shake up the way in which publishers do business and the way in which publishing revenue is collected. If ASCAP, BIEM, Gema, the PRS and the others can get their houses in order (see Chapter 12), writers really will have a genuine alternative to signing a publishing deal – assuming that they can live without the advances. Even if this isn't an alternative that writers feel that they'd wish to pursue, the increase in bargaining power should help set a trend for shorter-term contracts and royalty splits increasingly in the writers' favour.

a point on publishing contracts

You must ensure that you have the right to use your songs on your own web site and, if you can, on other web sites, such as your record label's. The best way to achieve this is not to grant the digital distribution rights in your songs to the publisher in the first place. At the moment, publishers are resisting this, so you'll need to build some kind of protection into the contract.

Ask the publisher to grant a free licence to you and your record company to allow you to use all of the compositions covered by the agreement, on both your web site and that owned by your label. Try and make the licence as broad as possible, so that streaming and webcasting are permitted.

Downloading rights will be hard to obtain – the publisher will want to keep control of the commercial exploitation of your music, and will probably only let you use your songs for promotional purposes. That said, though, your publisher is unlikely to object to the commercial exploitation of your songs on the net, provided that it's paid the going market rate.

web sites
for musicians

the power of the web

Today's musician is an entrepreneur running a business founded on creating and selling copyrights and generating economic activity from writing, performing and recording. The arrival of the internet gives musicians an opportunity to establish a base from which to grow all of these areas. Not only can bands set up their own web sites, linked to artists' sites of a similar genre, thus forging new communities of like-minded musicians, but artists can also use the web to access and research valuable information. In researching this book, for instance, I visited several music web sites, such as those run by music organisations like the PRS and the PPL and individual venturists' sites, from MP3.com to Hobomusic.com. All of them offered advice and information on issues ranging from online royalty rates to the role of managers. Some of this stuff is pretty basic, but it can still be a good starting point for leading artists up the right avenues.

why set up a web site?

Internet technology offers great opportunities for young, dynamic musicians, provided that a degree of control over this new technology can be gained for the musicians' benefit. And the first and most important thing that any young artist should do to ensure that he stays in control of his career is to set up his own web site, as well as to join or send his music to other people's sites (Peoplesound, Music Unsigned, etc). By establishing a web presence of their own, musicians give themselves the best possible chance of retaining an independent identity, even if they later sign to a record label.

Setting up a web site will provide artists with the opportunity to:

- Reach new markets and participate in new revenue streams;

- Maximise the potential of getting their music heard by as many people as possible;

- Establish links with fans and allow artists to communicate directly with them;

- Participate in online chats, webcast recording sessions and live performances;

- Offer exclusive downloads, sell T-shirts and other merchandise and announce tour dates, release dates and other news updates;

- Stay in touch with fans night and day, around the world. The web site acts as a beacon, broadcasting the artist's music across the globe.

creating your own music web site

To most people, web design is a bit of a black art, and some unscrupulous web page designers will charge you a great deal of money for what can often take them as little as a couple of hours to achieve (although, to be fair, there are plenty around who will do a very good job for a competitive rate). Still, it's a cost that few bands can afford at the outset of their careers, so here's an overview of how to set up your band's web site for yourselves.

registering a domain name

First, before you do anything else, as soon as your band has settled on a choice of name, you should register that name as a URL (Uniform Resource Locator), or *domain name*. You should do this even if you have no intention of setting up a web site in the foreseeable future, as this will give you the best possible chance of obtaining the rights in the domain name before anyone else can. It's also useful evidence to substantiate, if necessary, the date that you claim you were first using your band name in public.

Registering a domain name is fairly straightforward – provided that the one you want isn't already taken. You'll need to be on the net already, and then you can either contact your ISP and ask them to perform a domain-name search of your intended choice (usually in the format http://www.*myband*.com) or, if your ISP doesn't provide this service, go to a domain-name registration site, such as Internic or Nominet (making sure that the site is ICANN accredited first – see later). These sites will allow you to enter your chosen name and search under the various possible suffixes, of which there are currently five – .org, .com, .net, .co, and .gov – although several new ones are being created. The name search facility is free, whether you're using your ISP or a dedicated web site. If the name has already been reserved, you will either have to choose another or amend your name, possibly by altering the suffix. Alternatively, you could contact the owner of the reserved name and offer to buy it from them.

Once you have clearance to use your chosen domain name, you should proceed to register it by following the self-explanatory commands on the registration site. Registering a global domain (.com or .org) will cost you somewhere between £40 and £80 for one year's ownership, although longer periods are available at a higher price. Local domains, such as .co.uk, are cheaper to register.

When you have created your web site, you'll need to ask the ISP hosting the site to link your registered domain name to your site.

preparing the content of your site

Start by asking yourself the following question: what does a typical music web site comprise? The vast majority feature text, images, streamed audio, downloadable audio and hypertext links to other sites. Assembling the various components necessary to build a music site is a time-consuming and fairly complex process. Let's take a look at each component in turn:

Text

Most web developers today use what is known as a web authoring package, the most popular of which is Microsoft's Front Page. Authoring packages enable you to create web pages in the same way that you would create an ordinary document in Word. The web authoring package allows you to graphically design your site by placing pictures and text where you want, by formatting the text in the appropriate style (colour, font, case, columns, tables, etc) and, ultimately, by publishing it as HTML, the web's most popular programming language.

Images

All music sites contain the band logo and an array of images, from reproductions of album and single sleeves (usually on the discography page), band photos, concert stills and so on. There are two ways of placing photographs on the site: either the image will have been shot by a digital camera, in which case the information making up the picture is stored within the camera in digital format and can be downloaded to your PC using software provided with the camera, or a non-digital photograph can be scanned in from its source (a magazine cover, etc) with a scanner.

Having scanned your chosen image into your computer, the next stage is to manipulate and edit the image. By using a software application like Adobe's Photoshop (http://www.adobe.com), you'll be able to correct over- or under-exposed shots and crop material that you don't want to appear in the frame. Once you've got the image how you want it, save it to your hard disk in one of the popular image formats (.JPEG, .GIF, etc) and write it to a CD-ROM like you would any other (music) file.

Images can also be manually drawn with a paint package. Free packages can be downloaded from the net on a trial basis, and many now come pre-installed on PCs. The most popular is JASC's Paint Shop Pro, a free evaluation copy of which is available on a trial basis.

Downloadable Music

You can store music on your site in a variety of downloadable formats, but unquestionably the most popular is MP3. To make your own MP3s from CDs of your recordings, you'll need a piece of software called an encoder. You will recall from Chapter 3 that the process of taking a CD track and turning it into an MP3 file involves two stages: converting the digital information contained on a CD into a .WAV file and then encoding the .WAV data into MP3 format. Your encoder will take care of both stages of this process.

Streamed Music

Providing a streaming facility on your site is a useful way of allowing visitors to preview your music before deciding whether to purchase it. Again, the music will need to be uploaded into an appropriate format, such as MP3 or Windows Media Audio, and the industry standard for streaming is RealNetworks' RealAudio. You can purchase a development licence from RealAudio which will allow you to embed their software within your site. This will enable you to stream audio clips to listeners or whole tracks in RealAudio format.

writing and designing your site

This is probably the hardest part of all, and only you can decide how to best present your ideas. However, there are a few useful rules that you can follow to make the site as interesting as possible.

Layout and Content

Remember that usability is as important as content. Visitors aren't just looking to hear music; they want a sharp, clearly-laid-out site that is easy to navigate. The classic layout of a music web site normally encompasses the following elements:

- Home page with menu options;
- News section with all of the latest updates;
- Band biography;
- Exclusive interviews;
- Downloadable music;
- Streamed music;
- Reviews and articles;
- Discography;
- Competitions page;
- E-mail option;
- Links to other sites.

Articles should be informative and entertaining, like the site itself. To help you get an idea of how to design and plan your site, visit a few other artist or label sites that you think are well designed and easy to follow and examine their approach to displaying content. If you're impressed by what you see, make a note of the source code that the writers have used.

choosing an ISP to host your site

Finding the right host for your web site is very important. Your first dilemma is whether to go with a free ISP or one that charges for providing web space. The choice isn't as obvious as it seems, as a paid-for ISP will probably provide faster access (access to free ISPs servers can be slow, because you're competing with so many other surfers), higher uptime (ie the amount of time that the server is operational) and better support. These are all important factors in choosing the right host for your site. Other areas to consider are:

- E-mail hosting (so that you can get feedback and other useful data from visitors to your site);

- Access to a sufficient amount of web space. Remember, one three-minute MP3 track can take up approximately 4MB of web space. Therefore, you'll need considerably more than the default amount given away by free ISPs, which is usually in the region of 10MB;

- Domain-name registration services;

- Telephone customer support and after-sales care;

- Access to and availability of broadband connections;

- The ability to handle credit-card transactions (sales of records, merchandise, etc);

- Guarantees on uptime – ie guaranteeing that your site should be up and running 24 hours a day and that only essential maintenance work should interrupt this access.

Finally, keep an eye out for the regularly updated Top Ten listings in internet magazines for details of the best web hosting deals available from ISPs.

transferring your site onto the internet

You can run your embryonic web site locally for a while, on your home PC, before transferring it to your chosen ISP. In fact, it's a good idea to do this, as it can take a while to assemble all of the necessary parts and obtain the necessary clearances (ie RealNetworks' developments licence). When you're ready to go online, the final stage in the process of creating and setting up your band web site is the transferral of your finished web pages to the service provider that you've chosen to host your site.

To transfer the completed site, you'll need to log onto your host's web server using FTP (File Transfer Protocol), which comes automatically installed on later versions of Windows. Prior to transferring your site to your chosen ISP, you'll need to enter into what is known as a *hosting agreement*, which will govern the kind of service that the ISP will provide and at what cost. The areas in which it's important for the host to excel (see "Choosing An ISP To Host Your Site" on the previous page) should also be reflected in the hosting agreement. Reliability is a key factor in getting people to return to your site time and again. If the server is down even for an hour or two a day, you should be entitled to compensation. In fact, you should seek a commitment from the ISP to a minimum of 90-95% uptime.

Another factor to look for in the agreement is the ISP's ability to handle credit-card transactions in a secure manner. Your ISP should guarantee that transactions will be 100% secure. In addition to providing you with a user name and password to access your reserved web space, your ISP should also be able to provide some technical/fulfilment support – updating databases, processing orders and so on. Finally, ensure that your

ISP is obliged to update you on the number of hits (visitors) to your site on a regular basis so that you can monitor its popularity.

After transferring the initial content of your site, you will need to keep regularly updating it to ensure that it retains its credibility. To update your web pages, make the changes required locally using the web authoring package, as before, and then resend the files using FTP.

web sites – some legal and business tips

protecting your name/domain name

Your band name is your brand name. As with any brand, the more successful you become, the more value or goodwill is attached to the brand. Of course, the term "brand" can encompass a logo as well as name. Just think of the Jamiroquai logo, which is so instantly recognisable that it can adorn billboards or record sleeves without any need for words of identification. Protecting the brand is particularly important on the worldwide web. If someone else registers a domain name based on your name or brand, or uses your likeness, image or logo on their site, potential customers may be lost and the goodwill in the brand may be compromised.

However, the threat of *cyber-squatters* (people who buy up popular domain names and then offer to sell them back to companies whose real-world names are similar to, or the same as, the registered domain names) has receded of late. A recent ruling by WIPO (the World Intellectual Property Organisation) found against cyber-squatters who act in "bad faith" and have no intention of using such domain names in connection with any legitimate business. In this particular case, New Jersey outfit CPIC Net had offered to sell the domain names emiwarnermusic.com, emiwarner.org, and so on, to the nascent Warner/EMI Music venture for in excess of $1 million. (Quite why executives at EMI and Warner hadn't thought to register these names prior to announcing the joint venture was something of a mystery. Nevertheless, they got there in the end.)

The two best ways of protecting your brand name are:

- Registering it as a domain name as soon as possible. This process – described above – is straightforward and relatively cheap. It's worth registering variations on the name and registering under different suffixes, if you afford it – .org and .com, for example – to give you maximum protection. (Cyber-squatters, such as CPIC Net, usually register all possible variations);

- Registering your name as a trade mark or service mark (see below) in the UK – as your home market – and, if you can afford to, in the major territories (the USA, France and Japan). By registering your band name as a trade mark, you'll be in a stronger position to prevent others from using that name in relation to music-industry-based products in those countries.

In the event that your chosen domain name is taken and you believe that you have a legitimate claim to the name, you can appeal to WIPO or one of the other four ICANN-accredited registrars. (ICANN stands for the Internet Corporation for Ascribed Names and Numbers.) ICANN will invite the owner of the disputed domain name to a hearing to justify their ownership, and the organisation has the power to rule that the name should be transferred, depending on the outcome, which isn't always straightforward – Sting lost his claim when WIPO ruled that his name was a common term and that the person who had registered it had not done so in bad faith. In contrast, the estate of Jimi Hendrix was able to satisfy ICANN's requirements of a valid claim to the artist's name, and was awarded the rights to the domain name jimihendrix.com.

trade marks and passing off

In the previous chapter, we looked at the increasing interest that record companies are showing in the ownership of artist web sites and domain names. Just as artists are arguing that record companies should no longer automatically have total exclusivity over their material in the Internet Age, so labels are seeking to grab a slice of income from activities traditionally exploited by artists outside the scope of their recording contracts, such as merchandising and touring.

Many labels will seek to achieve this by gaining control of an artist's official web presence. If you register your domain name and further protect it as a legally recognised trade mark at the UK Trade Marks Registry, you will be making a stand for your independence and you'll also be putting your label in the invidious position of having to contravene trade marks legislation and/or be held liable for the common-law right of *passing off* if they attempt to set up a rival web site in your name. (Passing off is a legal action founded on the principle that no man may pass off his goods as those of another.) However, passing off may be difficult to establish if you're a young and unknown artist, as you'll have to show evidence that there is goodwill attached to your goods and services (ie the record-buying public will need to be already aware of your existence).

registering a trade mark

You'll need to decide which products or goods you'll be looking to sell under your trade mark. For registration purposes, goods and services are usually split into different classes. You'll need to ensure that you cover all of the various possibilities arising from the exploitation of your music, and this will normally entail registering your trademark (in the UK) in classes nine (records), 16 (printed material, such as posters and album sleeves), 25 (T-shirts and other clothing) and 41. At the time of writing, registering in one class costs £395. However, it costs less to register additional classes in the same application, so it's worth covering all bases in one go.

Once you've registered, you'll have the comfort of knowing that you've put the world on notice of your rights. If you need to take action for infringement, it will be quicker and easier to do so if your trade mark is registered. If your trade mark remains unregistered, you'll have to rely on passing off; but, as mentioned above, you'll need to prove that goodwill already exists in your name, which is difficult.

who owns content on the web?

From a legal perspective, operating a web site is a precarious business. A typical music site will contain a lot of information and material, such as music (available for download or streaming), artwork (album covers, photographs etc) and even articles and interviews, which the law views as forms of *intellectual property* – in other words, these photographs and songs, etc, are capable of being owned by someone. When posting such materials on the net, you need to ensure that you've taken all of the necessary steps to protect your rights in this intellectual property. By the same token, in building the content of your web site, you'll need to make sure that you don't infringe the rights of others.

So there are two main issues here: how to prevent others from using your content and how to make sure that you're entitled to use the contents of your web site. Let's look at each in turn.

protecting the content of your web site

Although web pages themselves probably aren't protected by copyright (unless viewed by the law as a compilation or database), the individual elements that make up those pages are protected. We'll take a more in-depth look at copyright law in Chapter 11, but for now you should know that:

- Written text and computer programs are protected as literary works;

- Graphics and photographs are protected as artistic works;

- Music is protected as musical works and sound recordings.

Nonetheless, you should always assume that visitors will freely use the content placed on your web site, unless you warn them otherwise. To help prevent such unauthorised use taking place you should:

- Use copyright (©), trade mark (™) and registered (®) symbols at the feet of articles, in photo captions and wherever else they're appropriate to alert users to the existence of your rights. A copyright notice should also be included on all material made available digitally, stating that no reproduction of the copyright material is permitted without your consent. A typical wording would be, "The contents of these web pages are © [*band name*]. The copying or incorporation into any other work of part or all of the material available on the web site is prohibited";

- Utilise encryption technologies to prevent unauthorised downloading of music. (The subject of encryption is also covered in Chapter 11);

- Incorporate clearly signposted terms and conditions that govern the use or licence of copyright materials, if appropriate. For example, you could say that content may be quoted, provided that the source of the quote is clearly stated and provided that such quotations don't form an extensive part of the article and that the original wording isn't amended or altered in any way. (Chapter 10 covers how to bring such terms and conditions to the attention of web users in a way that will bind them to their provisions.)

ensuring that you can use the content of your web site

It's stating the obvious, really, but you must ensure that you clear all rights in advance, or own or license all of the materials that you intend to use on your web site. If you're in any way restricted in your use of materials placed on your site, make sure that those restrictions apply equally to those visiting your site.

If you decide to commission a third party to design and build your web site, you should be aware that copyright law views the web designer as the first owner of the copyright in the design. Therefore, you should ensure that you obtain an assignment of all rights in the content – graphics, text, artwork and so on – used by the design company in creating the site, along with a waiver of the designer's moral rights. It probably won't be possible to obtain an outright assignment of the software code used to write the site (HTML, Java, etc), as a designer will often base his design for a site on features or building blocks which are proprietary to him. Nonetheless, you should still ensure that you can use the designer's work on a worldwide basis in all media. The price that you end up paying for the assignment or licensing of rights should be a one-off buy-out, allowing you free, unencumbered use of the site once it has been designed to your satisfaction.

One other point worth bearing in mind, in relation to web site construction, is the use of hypertext links. In order to maximise revenue and exposure, you'll need think about linking to specific sites, particularly other music portals, unsigned music web sites or online retailers, so that visitors can click on a "buy now" option that leads them directly to a fulfilment provider, such as Amazon or CD Now. In this case, you'll need to ensure that you've obtained appropriate consent from these third-party sites.

hypertext linking and framing

There are two distinct methods of connecting different web pages on the same site or different web sites: by hypertext link or by framing. It's important to be aware of the difference when constructing links from your site, as potentially grave legal consequences may arise from your choice of connection.

Hypertext links allow users to move from, say, site A to site B simply by clicking on the link. (This action is the equivalent of typing site B's address at the top of the browser and pressing Return.)

Framing, however, works by dividing a web site into sections which appear on the screen simultaneously. In such a situation, it would be possible to move from site A to site B without knowing it, because site B appears within the main frame of site A, which remains unchanged. When this occurs, there is a possibility that you, as the owner of site A, could either find yourself in trouble with site B's owners, because you haven't accorded them an appropriate credit, or at risk of liability from a third party if the content of site B is illegal (for instance, if MP3s are being illegally downloaded from the site). Given such risks, you should take care to clearly display a message disclaiming or waiving responsibility for the content of sites to which you link. You should also ensure that you credit the owners of third-party sites for content incorporated in your site.

privacy and data protection

Running an interactive site, where you're monitoring and asking for feedback from users (e-mails and customer orders for CDs, for example), will invariably result in you obtaining personal information about your fans. You'll almost certainly wish to build a database of names and e-mail addresses of all visitors to your web site in order to ensure that you can target-market specific promotions, tour dates and release information. Such practices should be fine, but you should be aware that you have a legal responsibility to treat any personal data you receive and/or store in this way in accordance with the provisions of the Data Protection Act, 1998, which came into force in the UK on 31 March 2000. Broadly speaking, your obligations under the Data Protection Act are:

- To notify the Data Protection Commissioner that you're operating a web site holding personal data, and of what you intend to do with the data;

- To ensure that all individuals sending personal data to your site consent to the holding or use of such data. To achieve this, you should publish a statement on your site that clearly sets out the information which the Data Protection Act requires to be disclosed and asks for the relevant consent. To be on the safe side, force your visitors to actively give their consent by creating an icon that has to be clicked before you can receive any personal data;

- To inform all visitors what their personal data will be used for. They should also be informed if third parties are going to use the data – for example, if a marketing company engaged by you intends to use the data for promotional purposes;

- To make visitors to your site aware of any invisible methods of data collection that you are employing (ie *cookies*);

- To tell visitors if their personal data will be sent outside the European Economic Area (EEA);

- To let visitors know what to do in order to correct any personal data that is or becomes incorrect, and to inform them how to obtain a copy of the personal data held about them.

If the above obligations appear onerous, bear in mind that, in as transparent a medium as the internet, the opportunities for misuse or abuse of personal data are that much greater than in any other. By complying with these regulations, not only are you ensuring that you're operating your web site legally, you're also giving the fans that visit your site peace of mind. You're more likely to build a database if visitors feel that the data they're submitting will be stored and treated in a responsible way.

a sample privacy policy

Below is an example of a privacy policy which I've seen used in similar form by numerous commercial web sites, and which I've adapted here to suit a band running a music site. Note how all of the elements required by the Data Protection Act have been incorporated.

This Privacy Policy applies to your use of the Transatlanticmusic.com site. Please read it carefully. We may occasionally amend this policy, and changes will be posted on the Transatlanticmusic.com site.

We are committed to safeguarding the privacy of our web visitors and complying with all relevant data protection laws. All personal information provided by you through your use of the Transatlanticmusic.com site will be treated as confidential, except where indicated below.

We collect information from our fans in order to help us provide a high-quality and effective web site. In order to enable you to download and/or purchase recordings from Transatlanticmusic.com, it is necessary for us to collect the personal details which you are asked to provide during the order process and to pass these on to our fulfilment providers and partners.

Your credit-card details are passed directly to our fulfilment provider. We do not currently store your credit-card details but may do so in the future in order to prevent fraud and to make your purchasing experience easier.

We may also collect personal details when you enter competitions or other promotions on the Transatlanticmusic.com site, which we will use only for the operation of the promotion, unless indicated otherwise.

We currently use only temporary cookies to assist in the operation of the Transatlanticmusic.com site, which are effective only for the period of time that a customer visits the site. We may in the future use permanent cookies, which will allow Transatlanticmusic.com to recognise a customer's browser when a customer returns to the site and enable us to offer a more personalised service. You may configure your browser not to accept cookies at any time.

We do not disclose information about your purchases or your individual use of the Transatlanticmusic.com site, although we do collect and disclose generic data relating to certain areas (ie segmentation of buyer groups, etc), from which individual customers are identifiable to commercial partners from time to time. By using the site and purchasing music through Transatlanticmusic.com, you are consenting to such use.

From time to time, you may receive additional information about us, including Transatlanticmusic.com special offers and updates. We may also in the future pass your details on to carefully selected third parties, who may inform you about products or services which you may find of interest. If you do not wish to receive such information (whether or not you indicated so during registration), or if you would like further details about the personal data that we hold about you, please e-mail us at www.Transatlanticmusic.com.

setting up and running an internet record label

tales from the music business part II

how to break a band on the internet – the Creed story

s there any reason why the record industry can't come up with a *Blair Witch Project* and hit paydirt with an internet-led promotional campaign? Well, in fact, it's already happened. Step forward, God-fearing American rock band Creed.

The Creed story makes for encouraging reading. The band's label, US independent Wind-Up, sold over 300,000 copies of the band's album *Human Clay* in the first week of its release on the back of a cleverly orchestrated internet promo campaign that left the majors drooling in the wake of its success. Sales were driven by an intense micro-marketing campaign that cost less than £30,000 in total and focused on the following areas:

- Fans were encouraged to preview every song on the album in advance;

- The promotion involved the web sites of eight major retail chains and around 100 radio stations, where fans could download the first single, 'Higher', for free;

- Online retailers were also given an additional exclusive track from the album available for streaming on their own web sites. The idea was to help retailers and radio stations drive traffic to their sites by previewing the new music to Creed's fanbase. In exchange, the music retailers who participated prominently displayed Creed posters in their high-street stores;

- Wind-Up promised that the band would play a free concert for the radio station that registered the highest percentage of listeners in their market downloading 'Higher', which encouraged stations to get behind the record;

- 'Higher' could also be downloaded for free from the band's own web site.

During the campaign, Wind-Up says that about 250,000 individuals downloaded the album's first single, many of whom they believe bought the album during its first week in the stores. The record annihilated all competition, its success contrasting vividly with superstar Garth Brooks's simultaneous release. In its first week, it beat Brooks to the Number One position in *Billboard*'s Hot 100, selling 50,000 more copies than the album released by Brooks, the USA's top-selling album artist.

In the run-up to its release, Brooks conducted a multi-million-dollar promotional campaign that included a prime-time television special on NBC and television and trade magazine advertising to hype the release. The album was also heavily shipped into the major retailers, such as Wal Mart, and was sold with huge discounts.

While the major record labels have established internet divisions, they remain concerned about how to protect copyrighted music on the internet and how much consumers should be charged for downloading singles. Although most majors now allow fans to preview snippets of songs for promo purposes, they're reluctant to let artists give away entire songs. Wind-Up, on the other hand, never had any intention of selling 'Higher'. In fact, the label consulted with technology experts for several months to figure out how best to give the song away.

This new breed of US indie labels are spending as little money as possible on traditional promotion techniques, such as trade and tip-sheet advertising, as these publications are never read by music buyers. Instead, they use the internet to enable the label to communicate directly with the fans.

Creed went on to sell four million albums over the next two years, more than U2, Smashing Pumpkins or REM during the same period, despite virtually ignoring MTV and promo videos altogether.

Wind-Up's aggressive web marketing strategy could serve as a model for how internet-based record labels will conduct marketing campaigns in the future. Until now, the majors have poured cold water on the idea that a band could be broken on the internet, and have happily promoted the idea that an artist needs a big record company in order to penetrate radio and MTV. The Creed story could provide the inspiration to change all that.

internet record labels

a new attitude...

It's a record label, Jim, but not as we know it. The internet is opening up all kinds of exciting possibilities for those with enough know-how and a little bit of venture capital behind them and who want to set up their own record label. And that record label could be about to take on a somewhat different form.

Alan McGee's Poptones label is probably the highest-profile example of a new wave of record labels that are geared towards nurturing and marketing talent via the internet. Such labels are characterised by a cavalier attitude to singles (ie, "Let people download them as MP3 files for free; if they like the single, they'll buy the album") and a cavalier attitude to pricing (ie the album is sold both on the high street and online at anywhere between £7.99 and £9.99).

Labels like Poptones will be able to sell albums at the magic figure of under £10 because they won't be taking the hit on selling singles, which – unless they're a big smash – have increasingly come to be viewed as loss-leaders, a necessary evil in order to promote an artist and their forthcoming album release. McGee calculates that he loses 20p on each single he sells – the more he sells, the more money he loses!

...and a new game plan

Internet record labels need to adopt a more flexible business strategy generally and integrate traditional ways of exploiting music with internet technology in order to evolve and be competitive.

The game plan should look something like this:

- Build catalogue;

- Marry traditional A&R methods of band selection to internet submission of new music from undiscovered artists;

- Canvass fans' opinions of new music;

- Brand the label heavily, both through traditional media (advertising in the music press and broadcast media) and on the worldwide web;

- Establish a direct mail/e-mail database and breakdown of customer demographics;

- Use downloads of both audio clips and complete tracks as free promotional tools, in MP3 or encrypted format;

- License catalogue to digital distributors and/or forge strategic alliances with large software companies and other key players in the digital marketplace;

- Promote and target investment opportunities from venture capitalists and investors who specialise in funding internet start-ups;

- Ultimately, attract funding and/or licensing possibilities from a wider range of internet companies which need content suitable for the net.

the singles club

If things go according to plan, as soon as a critical mass of catalogue has been developed, together with a strong brand name and a significant fanbase, the label will be able to exploit new internet-based opportunities for expansion.

Key among these will be the subscription-based internet music club. Remember the successful singles clubs of the late '80s, which offered fans the chance to buy exclusive, limited-edition vinyl releases, such as the Seattle-based Sub Pop label, which helped break Nirvana? The internet version will operate on the same principles but will combine this with the more modern, Sky Box Office approach of offering customers music on a monthly basis in return for a small membership fee, which may be payable either annually or monthly. The difference in this case is that the customer receives an unlimited supply of that label's music for his or her subscription fee but with an element of exclusivity built in (ie receiving special offers or exclusive mixes or bonus tracks from their favourite artists).

net advantages

Let's examine how using the worldwide web can give an internet-active record label advantages over its more traditional rivals:

- Customers can access the label's web site and order CDs directly from it, which significantly reduces the label's distribution costs;

- Customers can directly download tracks, live concerts and samples, and can participate in interactive services designed to promote the label and its artists, such as interviews, live chats, polls and competitions;

- Direct contact with customers allows the label to develop a finely honed database for future sales and targeted marketing, such as pre-release and touring information;

- The exclusion of various traditional middlemen – in particular, distributors and high-street retailers – allows for competitive pricing and higher profit margins;

- International orders can be received through web sites and e-mail;

- Financial transactions through the internet can be made secure and can be easily administered.

greater profit margin

The combination of the internet and powerful, inexpensive studio technology will make it possible for smaller companies to create and distribute new music cost-effectively. As a result, prices can be reduced and margins enhanced while music is distributed to a global audience.

cutting out the distributor

Historically, the power base of major record companies stems from their catalogues and their ability to distribute efficiently, often using an inhouse distribution arm (such as BMG Distribution Services, EMI Distribution and Universal Music Operations) or a jointly-owned distributor such as TEN (The Entertainment Network, jointly owned by Sony and Warner). Traditionally, independent record labels have had to out-source their distribution to a 3MV or a Vital, and, because of lower volumes, have allocated up to 25% or occasionally 30% of the wholesale price of a record to the distribution company. By using the internet as a means of direct distribution (on downloads, at least), the label's gross margin will be substantially increased.

cutting out the retailer

Not only do distribution costs decrease, but the retailer's margin (traditionally the biggest slice of the cake) may also ultimately be excluded from the equation.

Let's examine the differences between selling an album via the high street and via customer orders for the same record over the internet by using the price-comparison tables below.

Revenue

	CD SOLD AT RETAIL	CD SOLD OVER THE INTERNET
Retail Price	£14	£10
Dealer Price	£8.40	Nil
Retailer's Margin	£5.60	Nil
Discount To Retailer At 10% Of Dealer Price	84p	Nil
Net Sales Revenue	£7.56	£10

Costs

	CD SOLD AT RETAIL	CD SOLD OVER THE INTERNET
Manufacturing (per unit)	£1	£1
Mechanicals (per unit) At 8.5% Of Dealer Price	71p	71p
Distribution (per unit) At 25% Of Dealer Price	£2.10	£1
Total Costs	£3.81	£2.71
Profit Margin	**£3.75**	**£7.29**

As the above table shows, despite selling to the customer at only £10 over the internet, compared with £14 in the high street, the internet-fulfilled sales generate a profit margin nearly twice as high! Even though the cost of manufacturing the record is, of course, exactly the same (and presuming that mechanical royalties are calculated in the same way), the absence of the retailer's margin enables the label to charge its customers considerably less and still make a large profit.

There are a couple of things that you should bear in mind, however. The above example works on the basis that the distribution of orders received via the net is cheaper than fulfilling orders placed by shops, because the distributor doesn't have to factor in the massive returns privilege that most high-street chains will ask for. In addition, at the moment the ratio of high-street sales to internet sales is not 1:1; in fact, the success of the above model is wholly dependent on consumers wanting to shop for records on the internet. At the moment, we're a long way from online shopping being the norm, but the next generation of record buyers could change this.

how will the label operate?

Broadly speaking, sites that supply music on the net fall into two separate and distinct models: those that sell existing catalogue as retailers (ie CD Now and Amazon) and those that create new copyright from unknown bands, followed subsequently by the distribution of this music (ie Peoplesound, Channelfly, Vitaminic).

The new generation of internet record companies will tend to fall into the second category. However, in order to maximise their chances of success, labels should seek to embrace both models by using the net for distributing existing catalogue and signing new catalogue. They will still need someone to provide fulfilment of the physical orders taken over the net and, unless a coalition of labels funding a jointly-owned distributor is established, distribution will continue to eat into profits.

As downloads come to be of greater importance, distribution costs will fall and profit margins should increase, provided that the label has established an effective presence on the net so that people know where to find it and/or its fulfilment partners. And in order to achieve this, internet-based labels will need to spend a little money.

the costs of running a label

Internet labels should allow for the following areas of expense in starting up and running their businesses:

Internet Costs

These will include both the development of the label's web site and the cost of running and continually updating it. As we covered earlier, when looking at web sites for artists, the look and feel of a site is very important. It has to be user friendly and it has to be up to date, with new releases and up-and-coming events, such as tours, advertised in advance.

Marketing Costs

The promotion of the label's releases is usually the most expensive area of all in breaking a band, and the internet alone isn't going to be enough to do this. Advertising in the most visible media – ie the monthlies (*Q*, *Select*), the inkies (*NME*) and specialist magazines (*Mixmag*, *Kerrang!*) – together with tour support and radio plugging are all vital and effective methods of garnering attention for a new band. However, they all demand a considerable amount of money for their services. Internet-based promotion will also be useful, particularly banner and "pop-up" advertising on target web sites – online music retailers, music and lifestyle companies etc.

Manufacturing, Distribution And Artwork Costs

Traditional sales and distribution will still need to be channelled through established retail routes, and an established distributor – such as Vital or 3MV, which has major accounts with all of the major retail outlets and a strong, focused sales team – is going to be very important.

Recording Costs, Including Advances To Artists

Record labels are beginning to realise that they don't need to spend a quarter of a million pounds to record an album any more. The recent quantum leap in home studio recording technology and, indeed, its affordability (compare the price of samplers now with, say, three years ago) have had a huge impact in the cutting of recording budgets.

Legal Costs

Never underestimate these! Actually, one of the first things that needs to be considered is the registration of the label's name as a trademark at the UK Trademark Registry in the appropriate classes (usually nine, 16, 25 and 41). Labels will also need to have a set of precedent recording and licensing contracts drawn up, along with standard synchronisation and sample clearance agreements, producer agreements and so on.

Overhead Costs

The usual suspects – office expenses, travel, bank charges, insurance, rent, stationery, postage, salaries, accountants' fees, etc.

relations with artists

The new generation of internet record labels should be sure to read Chapter 6 of this book. They shouldn't go charging packaging deductions for downloads, for instance, or trying to claim ownership of their artist's web site. Young bands go to independent labels because either no one else will sign them or because the labels in question are cool and cutting edge, they allow a lot of creative input and they respect their artists. Presumably, labels want artists to sign to them because of the latter. They probably won't be signing because of the size of the advances on offer, so internet labels will need to be flexible in other areas (royalties on downloads, custom CDs and so on) while retaining enough profit margin to make the operation viable.

The financial relationship between the new generation of internet record labels and their rosters should be characterised by openness. Sales derived from the online and hybrid exploitation of product should automatically create transparent electronic records, so that all of the relevant data is visibly displayed to the artist on request. This practice will make the auditing of accounts more accurate, and should hopefully dispense with a cause of tension that traditionally exists between an artist and his label.

the run-up to a new release

Once a band has finished recording their album, the internet will be an important tool in the run-up to the record's release. Let's look at the classic record company model for breaking a record into the chart and gauge how the label can use the net to adapt that model and enhance its promotion.

Three months from LP release – The band master the record (in sequence, with edits, segues, cross-fades and so on) and the final cut is approved by the label. The lead single will be chosen from a shortlist. (In all probability, one or two obvious contenders would have surfaced during the recording and mixing processes.)

Ten to twelve weeks – The artwork concept for the LP is finalised and the artwork designer co-opted into the final choice. The artwork is then sent to the printers.

Nine to ten weeks – Test pressings and reference CDs are approved by the band. The proofs of the sleeve artwork are checked and approved.

Eight to nine weeks – Promo compilations and samplers featuring the best four or five tracks are prepared for the monthly magazines, with long lead times for reviews. The producers of terrestrial, cable and digital TV shows are sent preview copies of the single.

Six weeks – A fortnight before the album, the first single is released online as a free promotional download only, possibly in conjunction with a paid-for limited-edition physical release – for example, a three-track CD single featuring two exclusive tracks not on the forthcoming album will be available for physical distribution via the label's internet fulfilment provider. The single is sent out to journalists and reviews are staggered to coincide with publication or scheduled for the week prior to release.

<u>Five to six weeks</u> – The official label web site and band web site are updated to incorporate all of the news on the forthcoming releases. The album cover art and track listing are previewed. Online interviews and other features will be set up, with the band's participation. The single goes to radio and pluggers are used to try and get the record onto the weekly playlists in advance of release.

<u>Four weeks</u> – The "physical" single release is a fortnight away. At this stage, both the single and selected album tracks will be available as up to 60-second-long audio clips. The single may also be playlisted by internet radio stations streaming and webcasting to ADSL subscribers, WAP and broadband internet users. Data will be compiled to monitor the number of streams broadcast by internet radio stations and other online entertainment providers, and a national airplay chart for the internet (as well as mainstream radio) will be compiled.

<u>Three to four weeks</u> – The band's fanbase will be e-mailed with information about the forthcoming releases, with the single attached as a free MP3 file. Live shows will have been booked for this stage, timed to coincide with review deadlines, and these gigs will include a key London showcase for new bands or a headline London appearance for more established artists, coinciding with the filming of TV promos. Trailers and other printed advertisements appear in the press promoting the single. Racking, displays and other point-of-sale promotions are agreed with high-street retailers for the sale of the album, and the racking equivalent with leading online retailers (ie their home page displays in the week of the album's release) is secured.

<u>Two weeks</u> – The single is now officially released. Fly-posters and music-press adverts for the album start to appear. Banner advertisements and links appear on connected web sites (MP3.com, NME.com, etc) in order to draw music fans to the label's web site or that of its fulfilment provider. Orders for the album are taken over the net and in the high street.

<u>One week</u> – Album reviews appear in the weeklies and on web-based "magazines". Press, TV and live promo work converges around this period. The key live show takes place, with a simultaneous webcast previewing

new album material available for net users, or maybe only subscribers to specific sites.

Week of release – The album is now available as a simultaneous worldwide release in a leading secure format (ie Liquid Audio, WMA) for downloading at £9.99 and on the high street at £12.99 (possibly with extra tracks, and certainly with different packaging).

Post-release – Six months after the initial album release, and after having released a further couple of singles in the meantime, the label makes selected tracks available, with the band's consent (remember, this has to be secured in the contract), for instore and net-based custom CD manufacturers, possibly to coincide with sales promotions and tie-ins (for example, two LPs for £22). In addition, some or all of the tracks may be licensed to a digital distributor or a subscription-based content supplier and so on – the post-release sales and campaign opportunities are endless, if you have enough imagination and/or can predict where the next lucrative points of cross-fertilisation will arise. It isn't just a question of trying to tie in with some dodgy film soundtrack any more!

what's the future for indies?

"There's a huge groundswell of music being made that most people haven't even heard of, and for me that's very exciting... This is the best time for independent music since Mute first started, back in the late '70s..."
– Daniel Miller, label boss of Mute Records

Rumours of the indie scene's demise have been, to paraphrase Mark Twain, greatly exaggerated. Not the shoe-gazing, fey, jingle-jangle indie guitar scene, you understand (stand up Teenage Fanclub, Bluetones, Cast, Embrace etc) – we can all get by happily enough without pronouncements that veer from the clichéd inane ("We just make music for ourselves, and if anyone else likes it then that's a bonus") to the clichéd arrogant ("We're great, we are. We're mad for it. Our next single rocks more than The Stones," repeat *ad nauseum*). No, I mean the *indie* label scene. In fact, it couldn't be in ruder health. It's just that the traditional guitar-band culture has been replaced by a DJ-led alternative dance scene promoted by the likes of Basement Jaxx, Aphex Twin and Underworld, embracing garage, hip-hop and out-and-out pop. (Think of the wholly independently owned Jive's success with Britney Spears and The Backstreet Boys. Then again, perhaps not!) Even so, there's still room for guitar bands to cut through.

Witness V2's success with Stereophonics and Independiente's coup with Travis – both of these bands sold a lot of albums.

The current UK indie scene is very eclectic. Pop is no longer the exclusive domain of the majors, as Beggars Banquet, Mute, Jive and Edel have all shown. Dance music, meanwhile, has become big business, and thanks to the pioneering achievements of Ministry Of Sound the genre is now shifting prodigious numbers of albums, as well as singles. The difference is in the types of albums that are being sold. Okay, relatively few dance artists achieve prolonged album success (although Mute can lay claim to one of the biggest selling albums of recent years, Moby's *Play*), but Ministry have almost single-handedly taken the lucrative dance compilations business away from the majors and placed it where it belongs – in the centre of club culture.

the internet's role in the future of the indie label

So, how does the internet fit into all this? So far, as we've seen in this chapter and elsewhere in the book, one of the net's main advantages is that it provides indie labels with an opportunity to compete with the majors on a level playing field by utilising digital distribution to reach target markets and by cutting out the retailer's margin to increase profitability, hence giving the labels more money to reinvest in marketing their artists.

Corporate mergers – in particular the Polygram/Universal, AOL/Time Warner and EMI/BMG deals – will mean more space for independents rather than less. More bands are being dropped and more staff are losing their jobs as a result of the corporate pruning that goes on in the wake of these deals. This in turn means that more quality artists and experienced A&R, business affairs and marketing people are becoming available to be snapped up by progressive indie labels.

There are some tough choices ahead for independent labels, if they are to cut a swathe through the overcrowded marketplace of e-commerce and use the internet to expand rather than tie up their businesses. There are still too many small internet players offering tempting advances (and often shares) in return for exclusive distribution rights. In the next chapter, we'll look at how to get the best out of these kinds of deals, in particular how to ensure that various safeguards are built into a contract so that, if your internet partner goes belly-up, you can bale out.

It seems that the problem with the whole rationale behind these exclusive deals – the kind in which EMusic, Liquid Audio, iCrunch and others specialise – is that they miss the point of where music exploitation on the internet is heading: subscription. It's a word that keeps cropping up throughout the book, because in the overall mass of ideas, half-baked "visions" and general confusion surrounding the net, it's the one business model that seems to stand out as having the most chance of success. For a subscription-based music service to work, it will need a handful of huge content aggregators with the rights to distribute a vast selection of music to subscribers. You can already see that this is the direction in which the AOL/Time Warner alliance is heading.

If you're running an indie label and your catalogue is tied to, say, EMusic for the next five years, you may well miss out on several years' worth of net-based revenue derived from a popular subscription service, where your acts would benefit from being located on the same site as numerous other labels' well-known artists. That's not to say that, in the short term, a substantial advance (ie real money as opposed to a theoretical projection) in return for exclusive rights should be turned down; it's just that the options and trends need to be weighed up carefully before putting pen to paper.

Still, despite all of the confusion, it's against a backdrop of increased dynamism and success for the independent sector – of which even the majors are envious – that Poptones, Mudhut and others are launching the new wave of internet-embracing indie labels. The future's looking very healthy for the mavericks and entrepreneurs on the cutting edge of the music scene, for those who aren't afraid of change but can see the internet for what it is: a great opportunity to break into new markets and promote new artists and new musical trends.

indie labels – how to use the internet

tales from the music business part III

Alan McGee – from Creation to Poptones

Alan McGee is famous for discovering Oasis in a Glasgow venue back in 1993 and signing them to his hipper-than-hip independent record label, Creation, named after the psychedelic '60s band of, er, the same name. The label had already established a roster of cutting-edge indie acts before Oasis were signed, from the fledgling Jesus And Mary Chain to Ride, My Bloody Valentine and Primal Scream, whose magnum opus, *Screamadelica*, released in 1991, probably remains the landmark Creation release.

After Oasis, however, things started to go a bit pear-shaped creatively speaking, if not financially. McGee became wrapped up in the *bête noire* of late-'90s mainstream music culture, churning out product to satisfy radio programmers and MTV. He also made one or two questionable signings (One Lady Owner anyone?). However, the internet came to the rescue, reinvigorating McGee's love affair with the music business and leading him to quit Creation for the pastures new of Poptones.

McGee had taken Creation as far as he could – in 1996, Oasis were briefly the world's biggest-selling band, and it doesn't get any better than that, so the subsequent years at Creation were, inevitably, an anti-climax. And so to Poptones, a new vehicle with a new, net-friendly label concept. The whim of a bored millionaire increasingly coming to believe that he has the Midas touch, or a carefully planned, ingenious use of the marketing and exploitative opportunities provided by the internet? Time will tell. However, the move is of great interest in the context of this book, particularly as it marks a shift towards independence from major-label backing, a shift made all the more inevitable by McGee's disagreements with his former label's principal investor, Sony, over the role that the internet should play in the promotion of his artists' music.

In Creation's later years, McGee clashed with Sony over his plans to issue free MP3 downloads of tracks from the Oasis album *Be Here Now* prior to its release. Not unpredictably, Sony put the kibosh on such foolishness and similar giveaway MP3 ventures proposed by McGee. This divergence of opinion over the value of the internet and the way in which it could be utilised to promote Creation's artists made McGee see that it was time for a change, time to bypass the traditional and outmoded ways of doing business. As the new century dawned, the demise of Creation was announced and Poptones emerged from the chrysalis. As if to emphasise the severing of the umbilical cord with Sony, and to retain its independence, Poptones went to private investors in the stock market to obtain start-up capital rather than falling back on looking for funding from major labels.

McGee's first signings – amongst them El Vez, a gay Los Angelean masquerading as a Mexican Elvis, and Selofane 74, purveyors of daft analogue synth sounds – don't sound auspicious ("...all the people we're signing are lunatics, drug addicts or ex-drug addicts...").

Still, although one might question the musical vision behind the label, it's encouraging to report that the more artist-friendly "e-commerce contracts" that Poptones were touting are just that, despite having a striking resemblance to full-blooded standard major-label documents in many places. Artists are being signed for only a couple of albums; advances are low and all-in (ie inclusive of recording costs), so artists aren't constantly under pressure to pay off a large, unrecouped balance; and royalties have been simplified, with the removal of packaging deductions across the board, not just on downloads.

There is as yet no sign of a Poptones TV show, nor different web-based radio shows. Nonetheless, as McGee himself puts it, "When you get MP3 properly into people's homes, when they're listening to MP3 on their TV, then it'll go overground... The minute cable takes off, this is going to explode." The extent of the role which the net will ultimately play in the future of Poptones remains to be seen, but for now the label's net-friendly ethos and desire to operate without support from a major label is evidence itself of changing times within the music business. In the meantime, watch this space...

digital distributors' strategies

Whoever you end up jumping into bed with will have a significant impact on your online business strategy, even if they're only a relatively short-term partner. Although you'll still keep hold of the right to physically fulfil stock orders taken online, your business plans will be compromised if you choose weak or poorly considered partners in the area of electronic fulfilment. It is therefore critical – particularly for independent labels with only a few acts on their rosters – to examine the new distribution company's strategies, investment sources and marketing plans very carefully before taking the plunge.

More and more players are emerging in the burgeoning online market all the time, so many that its difficult to keep tabs on them all. Many of them will be chancers while a few will have some coherent strategies, but remember that they're all taking a gamble, to a greater or lesser degree – no one is able to predict how important digital distribution will be or in what ways.

some big-name tie-ups

To help you in your choice, let's have a quick look back at some of the deals that have already been struck:

- Rounder Records, one of the most prestigious independent labels in the US, signed a deal for a large part of its catalogue with Liquid Audio, who have established themselves as a leading player in digital music distribution;

- Cooking Vinyl – the UK independent whose roster includes XTC, Ani DiFranco and Billy Bragg – signed a digital distribution deal with EMusic;

- Beggars Banquet initially signed a deal with Liquid Audio to make around 2,000 digital tracks available in the US and then followed this up by becoming the first independent label to announce a subscription/flat-rate service in conjunction with MP3.com at the tail-end of 2000 in a deal which involved all of the Beggars Banquet imprints – Mantra, Mo Wax, XL Recordings, Too Pure and Wiiija – giving subscribers the opportunity to download and stream music from acts such as Prodigy, Basement Jaxx, Badly Drawn Boy and Cornershop;

- The independent dance labels Nuphonic and Ultimate Dilemma both signed to the UK-based company iCrunch, itself part-owned by EMusic;

- Critically lauded indie label Chemikal Underground (Delgados, Mogwai) also signed digital distribution rights exclusively to iCrunch.

licensing catalogue for online exploitation

what are the options?

Okay, so you want to license your catalogue to a digital distribution company. They are, after all, offering you a fair wedge up-front, or at least I hope they are or you shouldn't be doing the deal. Still, as we saw at the end of the previous chapter, before you take the money there are a few things you should consider.

In particular, you'll want to ensure that the rights granted are limited to the minimum possible forms of exploitation. Companies such as Musicmaker and CDuctive specialise in creating custom-made CD compilations, where consumers choose a number of songs by different artists and buy their chosen compilation tailor-made to order. This may be a possible way forward that will allow you to keep your digital download options open for the time being.

Alternatively, you could enter into a licensing agreement with a company such as EMusic or Liquid Audio for the download rights in your catalogue. When doing so, however, you should make sure that you retain the right to physically fulfil any customer orders taken over the internet.

how much of your catalogue can you license?

Before entering into an agreement for the licensing of your existing catalogue to a digital distributor, you'll have to undertake an exercise similar to that performed by a company selling its shares. Your business affairs team will have to undertake a process involving the analysis of every exclusive contract into which you've ever entered (*due diligence*). Below is a list of the main areas that you need to be looking at.

- The territorial restrictions in your artist contracts. Remember, it's up to you to put the onus on your licensee to ensure that they download to end users within the territory that you've specified to them for each of your artists.

- The royalty provisions in your artist contracts. Many of your older contracts (probably pre-'95) won't specifically deal with royalties on digital exploitation, but if you license an older artist's back catalogue then you'll have to pay them a royalty on any sales, and this may need some clarification. There is an argument that, as you've licensed rights to a third party (albeit digital rights that may not have been contemplated by your agreement), the artist should be paid a percentage of the net income that you receive from third-party licensees. Often, the problem here is that invariably such clauses are worded "…in respect of sales by licensees outside the UK…", which makes it tricky to account for downloads in the UK. Standard new-configuration royalty clauses won't be of any help, either, if they're limited to digital audio tapes, MiniDiscs and other audiophile recordings, as downloads don't fall within any of these categories.

• The right to compile and/or license to third parties. This won't be a problem in your recording contracts, but this may be subject to restriction if you've entered into a licence agreement either directly with an artist or with another label. If you don't have the right to sub-license individual tracks, you won't be able to enter into any agreements with custom CD manufacturers.

• Do you have digital rights to grant? This may be your most obvious concern, but it's not always an easy question to answer. However, it's more likely to be an issue in licensing agreements, which will often say that "…any rights not expressly granted to [you] are reserved by [the licensor]…" If your contract doesn't contain such a provision, or is silent on the subject, I would suggest that you take the positive view and grant the rights.

• Finally, on the subject of licence agreements, remember to check the term – your rights may already have expired!

You'll also want to consider renegotiating with major artists before sell-off in order to bring their digital rights on board and thereby increase the value of your catalogue, although this may not be an issue if a digital distributor has already made you an offer knowing that several artists are excluded from the licence agreement for one reason or another. You'll also need to find out if you're obliged to automatically license future artists to the digital distributor. More on this below.

the contract – how to protect yourself

Of course, your ability to negotiate the licence agreement will depend to some extent on your bargaining power. How valuable and sought after is your catalogue? Are there several players in the running? Whatever your bargaining position, however, the following areas of protection should be sought in all deals.

territory

Inevitably, given the nature of the internet, the distributor will seek worldwide rights for all licensed recordings. This is an acceptable request, but remember to incorporate a limitation for recordings for which you have only limited territorial rights, and specify these clearly in an attached schedule. In addition, clarify that future recordings will only be licensed to the extent that you have the right to license them.

You should try and put the onus on the distributor to take responsibility for ensuring that licensed recordings aren't downloaded in territories where you don't have rights. This is more problematic, and the distributor will fight hard to limit this provision, claiming that it is hard to police and that the situation is no different to CD Now or Amazon shipping worldwide to the consternation of local rights holders. Another, more persuasive proposal that the distributor may make is that, provided that the upload originates in the territory in question, it isn't liable for the ultimate destination of the download. You should resist these arguments; the distributor should be able to identify the territory in question, by virtue of either the consumer's credit-card billing address or his or her local ISP address, or both.

Also, as a breach of this clause is potentially significant, you should insist on obtaining a warranty from the distributor that it won't license recordings outside the territory of the agreement – or, at the very least, that it will use its best endeavours to ensure that this doesn't happen – and that it will be fully responsible for the financial consequences of such a breach.

term and product commitment

Most distributors will be looking for a term of three to five years. Given the limited revenues currently being earned from downloads, this is not an unreasonable request – it could be at least three years from the signature of the licence agreement before the distributor begins to recover its investment. You'll be signing an exclusive agreement, so it's essential to build in as many protections as possible in other areas of the contract in order to compensate for the length of the deal. Take particular note of the suggested buy-out provisions listed later.

The other key area here is the extent to which you will be obliged to automatically deliver new product to the distributor as and when it is delivered by your artists. To some degree, this will depend on the level of the advance and on whether advances are built in to be awarded on anniversaries of the contract or on delivery of additional product. The best possible scenario would be to limit this to additional recordings "added by agreement of the parties from time to time". You then have no obligation to deliver new product and are free to ask for further advances on delivery.

If you're obliged to deliver new product, ensure that it's only licensed for the unexpired portion of the term and not for a whole four or five years. Also, make sure that the distributor is obliged to decide whether to accept delivery within, say, a 30-day period, so that you're then free to license elsewhere if necessary.

streaming

Although you're granting the distributor exclusive rights to download your recordings for the duration of the agreement, you should try and grant streaming rights on a non-exclusive basis only. It's very important to grasp the difference between downloading and streaming. Downloading results in an identifiable reproduction of the downloaded track being stored on the end user's hard drive, while streaming is a transmission of the track which doesn't result in such a reproduction. It's a webcast, in other words, or the internet equivalent of a radio broadcast. It's not always clear when a contract is referring to streaming – it may use expressions like "digital audio transmissions" instead – but it should be implicit from the wording.

As mentioned earlier in the book, RealNetworks – the manufacturers of RealPlayer – has established itself as the market leader in real-time audio streaming, and at the time of writing is engaged in takeover negotiations with Microsoft, a company not slow to seize on a good business idea when they see one. Streaming rights could become particularly valuable in the future if the concept of pay per listen takes off as an accepted method of online delivery. You should try and retain the right to conduct non-exclusive deals with players specialising in this area, although this may be difficult. You should therefore ask on the basis that you need to retain the non-exclusive right in order to stream audio clips from your own web site for promotional purposes, as well as to enable your artists to do likewise.

advances

The level of the advance will depend to a large extent on the distributor's perception of the value of your catalogue, but this isn't always as black and white as it seems. Companies like EMusic have successfully floated on the US stock market and possess sufficient investment resources to enable them to stockpile as many copyrights as possible (at least, from the independent sector – they know that the majors won't play ball). Such a strategy will invariably mean that such companies are prepared to pay a premium rate to obtain the depth of catalogue that they know is required in order to become the number one player in their field. Accordingly, don't under-price yourself – even a relatively small specialist label could ask for $25,000 and upwards.

Of course, for the majors, the figures quoted in these kinds of deals will be in a different league, and anyway they'll almost certainly be something other than straight licence agreements. EMI acquired a stake in Liquid Audio as part of its agreement allowing Liquid Audio to digitally distribute a small part of its catalogue.

For smaller labels, however, it's critical to make these advances work. One option is to ask for a rolling advance, so that, as soon as the $25,000 advance is recouped, for example, the distributor is then obliged to pay another advance of $25,000 by the next accounting date. This kind of arrangement is well worth asking for, particularly as gauging the worth of a smaller label's catalogue at the outset of a deal is a lottery. In this way, you're rewarded if the deal has been successful for both parties.

royalties and royalty deductions

At this point in time, it's very unlikely that royalties will be expressed as a percentage of the actual download price or a notional "retail" price – there's simply no real understanding of what would represent a realistic figure, one which would allow the distributor its margin on the sale. Almost invariably, the royalty will be a percentage (usually 50%) of the distributor's net receipts or net revenues. It is how "net revenues" are defined – and limited – that will determine your royalty rate under the agreement. Legitimate deductions from the distributor's income should include:

- Transaction processing fees, such as credit-card transaction fees payable to unaffiliated third parties, if any;

- Sales tax (such as VAT), if any;

- Mechanical royalties and/or public performance fees directly attributable to the digital delivery, if any;

- Shipping costs, if any. Of course, there shouldn't be any for digital downloads!

Other costs that the distributor will want to deduct from its gross revenue will be internet referral fees ("bounties") and advertising costs. These are both areas that you should look to limit, as both are open to abuse. A referral fee is a commission paid to an unaffiliated third party who, through its web site or via e-mail, refers a purchaser of a download to the distributor. Advertising costs are, as you would expect, those costs incurred by the distributor in promoting the licensed recordings, for example by placing a banner ad on a search engine or on an online retailer's web site.

You should limit both of these to a maximum of 10% to 15% of the distributor's gross revenues on an artist-by-artist basis (ie the costs incurred with respect to one artist aren't charged against or *cross-collateralised* with those of another artist). Ensure that advertising costs, in particular, are directly attributable to your artist(s) and not to the distributor's web site generally. Also, they should only be rechargeable for banner ads and nothing less.

As in any licensing agreement, there will be a percentage of sales or downloads on a free or no-charge basis. You should make sure that the total number of free downloads permissible on an artist-by-artist basis is no greater than 5% of the total net revenue derived from the sales of the applicable artist's licensed recordings. You may also want to limit the distributor's right to stream, transmit or webcast any particular recording to a maximum of one minute only. (This will be long enough to allow audio clips to be broadcast for promotional purposes.) Any longer use should require your approval.

As mentioned earlier, the distributor is responsible for paying any mechanical royalties or public performance fees to the appropriate collection societies or bodies. Exactly how much will be paid and to whom is still very much a grey area, so ensure that the wording is open enough to cover every eventuality.

Finally, it's also worth mentioning that, even though streaming rights may only be granted on a non-exclusive basis, if the distributor receives income from streamed audio this should be split in accordance with the profit-share ratio for downloads.

bounties

Referral fees should cut both ways and, just as the distributor is entitled to deduct such costs from net revenues, so you should also be able to take your commission of 10% to 15% of the gross revenue earned from a sale "introduced" by you. There are two points to take note of here. Firstly, you should try and take off the commission and then divide the balance in accordance with the agreed royalty share. The distributor will argue that these costs should come "off the top". To illustrate how this will affect things, if an album is downloaded in its entirety for a total revenue of $10 and you take a commission of $1.50, on a 50/50 royalty share, the balance of $8.50 will be split at $4.25 for each party (assuming, for these purposes, that there are no other costs to deduct). Your total revenue earned by that download will amount to $5.75, whereas, if the commission comes off the top, your royalty will be only $5.00, as the cost of the bounty is borne by both parties.

Secondly, exactly what constitutes an "introduction"? Usually, the purchase will have to take place during one visit for it to count. In other words, the web visitor will have to pass directly from your site to the distributor's site. Whether he or she returns to your site, or whether your distributor's site is linked to or framed by yours (see Chapter 7), should be irrelevant.

accounting and audit rights

Any digital distribution company worth its salt should be able to provide you with a secured online account which you are able to log onto to view transaction activity at any time. The transaction activity should show the exact number of downloads for each artist on a track-by-track basis, along with the income and expenditure relevant to each download. Of course, this is one of the great advantages of doing business on the internet, and is one which should make accounting a lot less contentious. For instance, with the increased ease of accounting, there's no reason why the distributor shouldn't account on a quarterly basis. The distributor should also be able to pass on personal data, such as the e-mail address of the consumer, subject to any applicable data protection laws.

"Transparent" online accounting makes it harder to justify under-accounting, particularly if the margin is significant. You should ensure that the usual audit rights entitle you to recover the costs of the audit, as well as the underpayment, if there is a discrepancy of 5% or more on contested statements.

buy-outs and one-off exemptions

You don't want to be tied to the wrong distribution outlet for four or five years, as this is a risk, given that none of these new start-ups have been around long enough to command a reputation or a tried-and-tested expertise in the nuances of digital distribution.

More significantly, you should try and anticipate the possibility of entering into a label deal with a major. Label deals are a particularly important source of funding for specialist independent companies and, although the major will be looking to sell physical product – CDs, vinyl and so on – in the usual way, they will invariably want to obtain digital distribution and streaming rights as well. If you've already granted these rights to someone else, you could have scuppered a potentially lucrative source of revenue.

The ideal way to keep your options open is to propose that you can buy your way out of the digital distribution agreement by repaying the outstanding advance, perhaps with a penalty, if you wish to buy out of the deal within the first two years. In addition, you can agree to use commercially reasonable – and maybe even best – endeavours to try and exclude the digital distribution rights from the label deal in the first instance. However, if you can't get the digital distributor to agree to this get-out clause, you should consider very carefully whether you should do the deal in the first place. If you still want to go ahead, and you still can't get the distributor to agree to these provisions, at the very least you should ensure that you obtain an exclusion for one-off compilations and synchronisation requests. It would be inexcusable to lose these deals just because you couldn't grant non-exclusive download rights.

Both of these options may involve you agreeing to pay a percentage of the income that you've earned from the label deal or the compilation/synchronisation licence, although you should be able to keep this fairly minimal. An alternative route is to try and keep the licence non-exclusive, although even this isn't ideal, and the digital distributor is unlikely to pay out advances on such a deal.

A word of caution, though: if your corporate strategy involves entering into a label deal with a major distributor or record company, think very carefully before committing to an exclusive deal that will tie up your digital rights for up to four years. However tempting the advance looks, you may be shooting yourself in the foot. I can't emphasise this enough. It would be a nightmare to lose the investment and distribution of a major label just because you've signed away your download rights.

termination

Many of the digital distributors currently building copyright portfolios are taking a risk in doing so. They are prepared to go into the red knowing that significant income from digital downloads and streaming is still some way off, if it arrives at all. It's therefore critical that you ensure that you can terminate the agreement in the event that the distributor goes into liquidation or enters into an arrangement with its creditors.

custom CD compilations

Some digital distribution companies will try and obtain the rights to license your recordings for custom CD compilations in addition to obtaining download and streaming rights. However, this should be resisted unless they have expertise in this area and are prepared to pay an additional advance to justify the granting of these rights. It's also worth taking note of the aggravation that can be involved in attempting to grant custom CD rights.

In June 1999, EMI entered into an exclusive five-year licensing agreement with Musicmaker.com, whereby customers would be allowed to produce their own custom compilation CDs. However, after concluding the deal, it came to light that the standard coupling clauses in EMI's recording contracts with its artists restricted "multi-artist compilations" without the artists' consent. The deal had to be held up while consents were sought, to the understandable annoyance of Musicmaker.com's investors, who promptly sued EMI. Even the majors can be caught out by the difficulties of adapting established contracts to new forms of distribution.

tales from the music business part IV

Ministry Of Sound – using the net to break overseas

"There's no access to dance music on the radio [in the US] and no dance singles sales. We believe the dance explosion is coming, and that it will come via the internet."
– Matt Jagger, MD, Ministry Of Sound

If Poptones is the blueprint for the indie record label of the future, Ministry Of Sound is the indie-label success story of the present day. And it's a success that isn't just confined to the UK.

Ministry's expansion into the US market has been made considerably easier by the success of its web site (http://www.ministryofsound.com). The first US album release, *Trance Nation America*, came on the back of phenomenal interest shown by US dance music fans, who account for nearly 40% of all visitors to the Ministry site thanks to the absence of any coherent dance scene in the US.

UK rock bands are forever bemoaning the difficulty of breaking the States, which involves endless tours, meet-and-greets with inane PR people ("Hi, Artie

Fufkin, Polymer Records. I go back with you guys…"), guest slots on innumerable radio stations that always have the letter K in their name for some reason and, of course, constant travelling from city to city, coast to coast. The US is a very big country in which to be undertaking a promotional tour, and many bands go a bit loopy on the road: they get sick of each other's company in the tour bus, they become demoralised playing to audiences a quarter of the size of those that they're used to playing to back home and, worst of all, they have to do all of this again and again before US radio stations finally start to pick up on them.

Therefore, the internet is a breakthrough in breaking the States, particularly for the dance music scene, as it does away with the vast expense and hassle involved in actually going there. For Ministry, who have a strong brand name associated with cutting-edge dance sounds across the world, their web site is the key to creating interest and building a buzz by providing downloads and live webcasts of MOS club nights.

the secret of their success

Ministry Of Sound aim to make the radio show, magazine, club and internet site work together as one. The impact of the web site thus far demonstrates that the plan is working:

- 60% of visitors to the web site are from overseas;

- Artists like Artful Dodger are heavily downloaded outside the UK;

- As a form of global mass communication, online promotions aimed at the core market of 16-22-year-old dance fanatics are very effective compared to promotions in traditional media (known as *offline promotions*);

- Club webcasts attract thousands of users who are unable to attend the real thing – again, many of whom are located outside the UK.

So, why has Ministry's web site been so successful? What can other independent (or, indeed, major) labels learn from their achievements?

- The respect from its fanbase and the power of the Ministry Of Sound brand name is largely responsible for the impressive tally of site hits;

- They use incentives to persuade people to return again and again, such as mailing e-flyers to subscribers each week, advising them of special offers, new releases and promotions;

- They sell their own product online at a lean price;

- Their site is well designed – exciting and colourful in look and feel;

- Fulfilment of customer orders is quick and efficient.

To date, Ministry has adopted the approach of setting themselves up as being a single beacon in London broadcasting to the world. In the future, it may be that, in order to drive expansion, they will need to set up several localised web sites, thus establishing the same kind of attitude and expertise on the ground in other territories. A flexible and forward-looking outlook is essential.

internet law – how to do business on the net

your attorney advises...

So, you're going to be broadcasting DJ mix sets from Ayia Napa, selling reissue Undertones 7"s and sawn-off Metallica T-shirts, promoting next summer's Glastonbury Festival (even though you don't know the line-up yet) and auctioning exclusive sweat-stained Axl Rose bandannas to the highest bidder. You plan to do all this over the internet. You're going to be running a web site, or maybe several. Oh, and you've promised to deliver all this fab gear to your customers within seven days, or their money back, guaranteed.

Welcome to a legal minefield! Whether you're a band, a small independent label, an absolutely huge and not-very-independent-at-all label or a specialist web "e-tailer", you're going to need to know a little bit about the law if you intend to do business on the internet. That said, however, the Internet Age is a bit like the US gold rush of the 19th century – characterised by lawlessness!

When technology leaps forward in great bounds, it's often the case that the law is left lagging behind. In cyberspace, there are no obvious geographical boundaries and music travels freely across the globe in intangible form, so how do you expect us poor lawyers to cope? Still, do not fear. In the spirit of Hunter S Thompson's ever-helpful attorney in *Fear And Loathing In Las Vegas*, what follows is all the advice you'll need in order to make sure that you avoid falling into a worldwide-web-sized black hole.

before you start selling music on the internet

Successful retailing isn't just about understanding the laws that affect you. As you assume the new role of online retailer, you'll need to be clear and certain about the law in order to be able to deal effectively with customers. In particular, if you're engaged in transacting business over the internet, you'll need to arm yourself with the know-how to put in place the traditional mechanisms of a successful consumer-driven business transposed to a new context, including effective pricing structures, handling capacity for secure credit-card transactions, delivery and distribution of customer orders, stocking and warehousing of goods, customer relations and methods for responding to customer complaints, dealing with exchanges, returns, faulty goods and so on.

the key areas of internet law

Law in the UK is adaptable and flexible. It's not afraid to look to the past – to laws laid down through centuries of common usage and the decisions of the courts in past cases – for inspiration. As mass-media guru Marshall McLuhan once said in one of his more prescient moments, "We look to the future through a rear-view mirror."

That's probably as good a starting point as any for looking at the way in which the law tackles the challenge of new technology. The courts look at the problems posed by web sites, domain names, ISPs and so on and apply real-world analogies. Also, many existing laws – both national and international – already apply, or can be readily adapted to apply, to the internet.

contracts on the internet

Although the technology may be new, our existing legal framework – in particular the law governing the formation of contracts – can be used to solve many of the problems that those offering goods and services for sale or other commercial use over the internet are likely to face. If you're about to start trading online, you'll probably want to know the answers to the following (legal) questions:

- When do I have a valid contract with my customer?

- Which country's law governs my contract?

- If a customer in the States orders a CD from my web site, can they send it back if they don't like it?

- Can I add the personal details that I've been given by my customer to my artist database?

- Can I issue standard form contracts that override my customer's rights?

- If so, how do I know if my customer has agreed to my terms?

when is the contract formed?

In English law, a contract is formed when there are outward signs of agreement between the parties. Once an offer (ie a statement of willingness to be bound on given terms) is made, an acceptance is all that is required to complete the agreement. Acceptance happens when there is acquiescence to the terms of the offer, and it must be absolute and unconditional. If the agreement is supported by an intention to create legal relations and *consideration* (a technical term for the price of the agreement, usually money or the performance an act), there is a binding contract. After the moment of agreement is reached, the parties are bound and it's then too late for either party to impose terms on the other.

That's the theory, anyway. Applying it to the purchasing of a CD over the net should illustrate how these rules work in practice.

Suppose a music fan surfing the net comes across CD Now and decides to order a CD that isn't available in the UK. The CD Now web site is a virtual shop window displaying graphics and information about pricing, stock, etc. By analogy with an ordinary high-street record store, the information displayed on the web site by the supplier is probably what is known as an *invitation to treat*, a stage in negotiations at which offers are invited and which is of no binding consequence in itself.

I say "probably" because web sites usually fulfil a dual function: they are simultaneously displaying and selling their wares. In other words, it's difficult to split the advertising of the CD with the sale of the CD. This has never been in issue for traditional retailers – if HMV are holding a sale and the latest Madonna album is displayed in the shop window at a heavily discounted price to promote the sale, it's quite possible that all sale stock has already been snapped up. It would be unreasonable for a customer to insist that HMV should re-order at the discounted price – hence the invitation to treat doctrine, which places no legal obligation on HMV to sell at the price in the shop window.

With the internet, however, this approach may not work, as it's technically possible for a web site to be constructed so that, once a particular item is out of stock, the offer to sell that item is automatically removed. As there are no decided cases addressing this issue, it's therefore advisable for a record company trading online to clarify on its web site that it won't be bound by any communications from potential customers.

However, it's likely that courts will view web sites as analogous to "real" record stores (remember Marshall McLuhan) and therefore construe that the graphics displaying the CD covers and their prices constitute an invitation to treat.

Continuing our example, when the customer clicks on the "buy this CD" icon, he or she is making an offer (admittedly on terms drafted by CD Now), which will be effective when received by the supplier. Once received, the order is sourced in the States and the CD is then shipped to the customer. A general rule of contract applicable to even the most modern methods of communication is that acceptance is only effective when the person who made the offer – in this case the customer – receives notice of the acceptance. In other words, only when the goods arrive in the UK at the customer's address is he aware that his offer to purchase has been accepted.

At this point, a binding contract comes into existence. The significance of this is two-fold: first, the customer is legally entitled to change his mind and cancel his offer to purchase at any time before the CD arrives, provided, of course, that he communicates this change of mind clearly and unequivocally to the supplier (CD Now); second, the law governing the contract is that of the country in which the customer makes the offer – in this case, the UK.

Indeed, the customer can change his mind not only before the CD arrives but also after. New legislation – the Directive on Distance Selling, which we'll look at later in the chapter – provides for a seven-day cooling-off period for a customer dealing as a consumer in the EU. This will be applicable even though the supplier is based outside the European Union, as in this example.

what should you do?

You must be aware of the issues raised by the courts in adapting the principles of offer and acceptance to internet transactions. In particular, you should:

- Build a clear demarcation of responsibility for dealing with the cancellation of customer orders into your contracts with fulfilment providers;

- Set reserves against credits and returns at realistic levels;

- Ensure that, if you leave the day-to-day running and upkeep of your web site to a third party, the third party is responsible for displaying all of the necessary notices stating your customer service policies.

how is the contract made?

The contract involving the purchase of the CD described above was concluded electronically. When the customer clicked on the purchase icon on the screen, he was indicating that he wanted to be bound by CD Now's terms of sale (ie price and delivery time). These days, for most types of contracts, a handwritten signature on paper isn't essential, although there are a few that still require the quill-and-parchment treatment.

Cybersignatures, as they've predictably been dubbed, can also take the form of a PIN or a typed name at the end of an e-mail. With new legislation on its way (the Electronic Signatures Directive), contracting online is going to become much more common in the next few years.

how to incorporate standard terms into a contract

How can you ensure that your standard terms and conditions are incorporated into your contracts and yet don't put off potential buyers by making them scroll through pages and pages of small print before making their order?

Bear in mind that the terms of the contract need to be brought to the customer's attention before the contract is concluded, even if not necessarily read. The safest way to ensure that this happens is to set them out in full and force the customer to read through them and acknowledge them by clicking on a particular icon before he can proceed with his order. This is rather clumsily known as a *clickwrap contract* (after shrinkwrap, which made sense in the context of delivering software in that, once the packaging had been opened, this implied that the supplier's terms and conditions had been accepted).

However, the need to ensure that the terms and conditions are clearly displayed must be balanced against the need to offer an attractive and simple web page layout to the customer. The best of both worlds can be achieved either by creating a hypertext link to the front page of the web site, clearly marked to show where the terms and conditions can be found, or by pointing the customer in the direction of your FAQ (Frequently Asked Questions) page.

You should ensure that the customer's mouse clicks on an icon to demonstrate that he or she has accessed the relevant page prior to placing his order. In this way, the front page(s) of the web site are left as free as possible to fulfil your marketing team's innermost fantasies!

which laws apply? (the jurisdiction problem)

From a commercial point of view, the internet's globe-straddling potential is great news for the music industry. The door to free trade is now open to countries the world apart, both culturally and geographically. There has never been a better opportunity for selling Gentle Giant back catalogue in equatorial Africa!

Alas, from a legal point of view, the ability to reach customers worldwide is a big headache. You'll be contracting with people in hundreds of different countries, each with their own laws and ways of doing business.

One approach to this problem is to state in your standard terms and conditions that "this contract is governed by UK law". This should be fine in a business-to-business contract, but if a customer deals as a consumer – even if he or she acknowledges acceptance of your terms – this doesn't guarantee that these terms will automatically apply. Consumer laws exist to protect customers from big businesses imposing their rules and regulations.

In the European Union, consumer protection laws have the power to override a non-EU company's terms of business. US internet retailers, such as Amazon and CD Now, know that the EU is hot on consumer issues and that an EU citizen will be able to rely on his or her domestic consumer protection legislation regardless of what their contracts say.

Aside from the consumer angle, there has been considerable confusion over which country's laws take precedence in any particular online communication or web site. The newly-finalised E-Commerce Directive dictates that online services will be governed by the country in which the supplier is established, with the term "established" in the Directive meaning having premises and staff. Simply locating a server in a particular country won't mean you're established in that country.

what should you do?

When faced with powerful domestic consumer laws, there's not much you can do, other than ensure that you're aware of and comply with the relevant legislation. You should seek advice on this before establishing your customer relations policies with a specialist consumer law practitioner.

distance selling

The soon-to-be implemented European Directive on Distance Selling is relevant to all contracts concluded by online consumers and retailers, including any record companies fulfilling that role, as these are contracts for the supply of goods and services between suppliers and consumers using "distance communication means". The regulations contained in the Directive should have a limited impact on online music retailers – the key rights, listed below, should already be standard in the terms and conditions of most reputable retailers.

Consumers Have A Seven-Day Period To Withdraw

The main thing to be aware of is that the Directive gives the consumer a right to withdraw from the contract until up to seven days after delivery of the goods without giving reasons and without penalty, although this won't apply if it would be unfair on the supplier for it to withdraw. However, the Directive isn't meant to be a charter for home taping. Records and other music products that have been unsealed by the customer cannot be returned under the cancellation rights. Online retailers should therefore ensure that they ship out only sealed products as part of their online mail-order selling operations.

You Must Fulfil The Order Within 30 Days

The supplier must fulfil the terms of the contract within 30 days of receiving the customer's order. This latter provision can be varied by mutual agreement but is nonetheless a tough provision for suppliers to abide by. In practice, though, consumers are more likely to rely on suppliers' own guarantees and customer relations policies in the event of problems arising, at least in the first instance.

Consumers Need Clear Information

As consumers cannot actually see the goods that they're ordering, you have to give them as much information as possible in advance, such as information concerning price, delivery costs, identity of the supplier and main characteristics of the goods, and all of this information must be given in a clear and comprehensive manner. If you intend to sell records, complete track listings should be included, if at all possible. It's now easy to obtain Japanese versions of CDs (always with bonus tracks) from the net, as well as a proliferation of mid-price or budget-price compilations under different titles, although with the same track listing. The scope for consumer confusion is vast.

advice for ISPs

can ISPs be held liable for someone else's actions?

ISPs and online service providers are an important part of the online music revolution, as the AOL/Time Warner merger showed. Record companies and music publishers may also find themselves fulfilling the role of an ISP if they branch out into offering online services direct to their customer base.

For anyone fulfilling online services, there is one very important legal issue to observe. As an internet service provider, you are vulnerable to the actions of others and face being held liable for acts done by third parties subscribing to your services or otherwise placing material on the internet – for example, bootleg MP3 files. This begs the question, should ISPs be held liable for acts which may well be beyond their control?

There are two main areas of potential liability for ISPs – defamation and copyright infringement – and there are also two new EU Directives in place to deal with these issues, the E-Commerce Directive and the Copyright Directive, although the latter is still in the pipeline. Unfortunately, as will become clear, the Directives contradict one another on the issue of ISP liability. However, these contradictions arise only with respect to liability for copyright infringement. On the subject of defamation, the law now appears to be fairly clear.

defamation and the Demon Internet case

A defamatory article was carried on Demon's server and read by a Mr Godfrey, who claimed for libel after he had put Demon on notice that it was carrying the defamatory material.

In the USA, the liability of ISPs for carrying material on their network is very limited. In the UK, however, ISPs are classified as publishers, and will be taken to have published material even if they are ignorant of its defamatory content.

There is, however, the new defence of *innocent dissemination*, which is included in the Defamation Act. Provided that the ISP takes reasonable care, and doesn't know or has no reason to believe that what it did caused or contributed to the publication of a defamatory statement, the ISP will escape liability. In this particular case, Demon were put on notice. Once this occurred, the onus was on Demon to remove the offending material from their network. They did not, and were held liable for damages.

what can ISPs do to stay out of trouble?

ISPs must make sure that they act quickly to remove access to information upon obtaining actual knowledge that the information in question may be defamatory, or ensure that it has been disabled at source (ie at the initial place of transmission). If they are sued, they should then be able to rely on the "internet defence" of innocent dissemination.

what does the E-Commerce Directive say?

The Directive, which was finally adopted by the European Parliament on 4 May 2000 for implementation in member states within 18 months, dictates that service providers will have no liability when they only provide access or transmission services – if they remain passive, in other words. If the ISP takes an active role – for example, hosting a web site – it won't be held liable for the content of that web site, in common with anyone else hosting a web site, as long as it is unaware of any offending material and it moves quickly to remove that material once put on notice.

Specifically, the Directive divides the issue into three areas: conduit, caching and hosting.

Conduit

ISPs won't be liable for information transmitted on their networks, provided that they don't initiate the transmission, they don't select the receivers of the transmission and they don't select or modify the information in the transmission.

Caching

ISPs won't be liable for the automatic, intermediate and temporary storage of information performed for the sole purpose of making the onward transmission of the information more efficient, a process known as *caching*. This exemption is aimed mainly at legislation concerning data protection, as personal data is very open to misuse, although the existence of cache copies is also a significant copyright issue, which we'll explore in the next chapter.

Hosting

ISPs won't be liable for hosting a web site provided that they don't have actual knowledge that the activity is illegal and, upon obtaining such knowledge, act swiftly to remove it.

Note, however, that ISPs may still be slapped with an injunction preventing them from performing any of the above (ie the hosting, caching or conduit of infringing information).

what does the Copyright Directive say?

The Copyright Directive is covered in more detail in the next chapter, but on the issue of ISP liability it dictates that temporary acts of copying – such as cache copying – are absolute exceptions to copyright infringement. In other words, an ISP's activities cannot give rise to a copyright infringement.

Where the E-Commerce Directive tries to put the onus on ISPs to ensure that infringing material isn't disseminated on the internet, the proposed wording of the Copyright Directive allows ISPs to wash their hands of any responsibility. As we shall see, the drafting of the Copyright Directive is therefore something of a triumph for the telecommunications industry.

piracy and copyright

how is the music industry combating piracy?

real-world piracy

Historically, piracy has always been a huge problem for the music industry. Piracy in relation to physical recordings – counterfeit and pirate records and bootlegs – deprives the industry of upwards of 75% of its income in some parts of the world, the Far East and Eastern Europe in particular, where copyright laws are weak and little attempt is made to enforce them. (In fact, one of the few countries in which Mainstream achieved popularity was Poland, for some bizarre reason. We were big enough to headline festivals there but, despite our album going out via Sony's SINE network, it was never going to sell more than a couple of thousand copies. Poland's major acts sell 30,000 albums a year, if they're lucky; the vast majority of record sales are bootlegs.)

Even countries like the UK and France – which have strong copyright laws – suffer from piracy, as anyone who has ever taken a stroll through Camden Market on a Sunday will testify. As a barometer of the sea-change in the industry, it's interesting to note that illegally-copied MP3 disks are now taking over from traditional CDs as the anti-piracy units' priority target. This isn't so surprising when you consider that, in the past, bootleggers had to have access to a small manufacturing warehouse in order to replicate CDs. Now, most MP3 product is knocked out in people's bedrooms.

Physical piracy – in the form of manufactured CDs and disks copied with MP3 material – remains difficult to stop, although the IFPI (International Federation of the Phonographic Industry) have succeeded in targeting and shutting down illegally operating CD-manufacturing plants in the Far East. However, although the problem of physical piracy remains a very real one, it is a manageable and identifiable threat. This threat is combated through a mixture of strong-arm tactics, vigorous crackdowns on bootleggers and strong copyright laws, which in the UK allow victims to sue for damages for copyright infringement and/or obtain an injunction in the civil courts; to involve the police in a criminal action, for serious cases of copyright infringement; and to bring a private criminal prosecution against the perpetrators.

The law has an impressive array of weapons at its disposal to combat physical piracy. Online piracy, on the other hand, is a different case altogether – more difficult both to police and prevent.

virtual-world piracy

"Some companies operating in the area of the internet may have a misconception that, because their technology is somewhat novel, they are somehow immune from the ordinary applications of laws of the United States, including copyright law."
      – Judge Jed Rakoff, presiding over Universal's lawsuit against MP3.com

The rumour and reality of piracy consistently undermines the development of music distribution over the internet. The major record companies in particular remain reluctant to upload their catalogues for fear of what might happen once their music becomes openly available for digital download.

The record industry is faced with a threat of online piracy operating on two fronts: one comprising PC and music enthusiasts, high-school kids in US college dorms innocently trading their favourite artists' music by e-mail; and the other involving file-sharing and pirate web sites offering downloads of copyright material, usually on a no-charge basis, profiting instead from advertising revenue.

The fact that MP3 files can be easily passed between individuals' computers as e-mail attachments isn't the only worry for the industry. Of possibly greater significance is the fact that there is nothing to stop a bootlegger legally purchasing a CD by, say, Michael Jackson, inserting it into his PC's CD-ROM drive, ripping the tracks and making them freely available as MP3 files on his web site. (We covered ripping in Chapter 3.)

Faced with these threats, the record industry in the States has not been slow to litigate, although thus far court action has brought mixed results. In addition to the RIAA case against Napster, the US recording industry's representative body has been involved in two other high-profile actions.

RIAA vs Diamond Multimedia Systems (1999)

In 1999, the RIAA brought an injunction against Diamond Multimedia to try and prevent the sale of their portable MP3 player, the Rio, but lost the case on appeal. The thrust of the RIAA argument was reminiscent of CBS's lawsuit against Amstrad Electronics some ten years earlier. In both cases, the music industry attempted to prevent the sale of stereo home recording equipment (in Amstrad's case, tape-to-tape recording machines) which the RIAA, as CBS before them, alleged encouraged mass unauthorised duplication of music, without payment to the rights holders.

In both cases, the record industry was unsuccessful. Amstrad didn't market their player as one which allowed the user to make unlawful copies of recordings, and as the player also had a lawful purpose – the making of copies for private use – the company was entitled to continue selling it.

RIAA vs MP3.com (2000)

MP3.com felt the wrath of the US recording industry for creating tailor-made custom CD compilations to customers' specifications (the MyMP3 library). They faced legal action because they held these compilations online, in a virtual locker, so that they could be listened to at any time by users. MP3.com found themselves in breach of copyright because holding the tracks online, and therefore making them available for download, was an unauthorised use of the compositions. MP3 intended to appeal against the court's initial ruling, but ended up settling the case with the BMI (Broadcast Music Inc), which enabled them to license the compositions legitimately.

Outside the law courts, the industry is looking to combat the threat of piracy in two ways. The proposed Copyright Directive and Electronic-Commerce Directive are the legal response to the threats posed by piracy while, alongside the protracted drafting of this legislative framework, the record industry is also working towards developing a technical means of preventing unauthorised copying and piracy.

the Secured Digital Music Initiative (SDMI)

The record industry wants to build a legitimate business in cyberspace, and it hopes to achieve this by way of the SDMI, which was touched on briefly in Chapter 2.

Launched by the IFPI and the RIAA in 1998, the SDMI aims to achieve two primary goals: to build a specification for portable devices, and to develop a broader specification for the electronic delivery of music. The idea is to promote copyright protection through ensuring that recordings are properly licensed by their owners and through developing secure envelope, watermarking and encryption technologies.

SDMI is very important to the record industry. Without it, piracy could escalate beyond the industry's control. With a successful specification, MP3 will be marginalised because legitimate content will be easily accessible. Yet, despite the increased resolve of the industry to combat piracy, SDMI is still some way short of achieving its stated aims. The encryption technology favoured by SDMI – like the legislation designed to protect the interests of copyright owners – is still reacting to, rather than dictating, the development of online music delivery.

what is encryption?

An encryption algorithm converts plain text into unreadable cipher text (encryption) and vice versa (decryption) using a special secret key. It sounds impressive, but the problem with encryption is that third parties are able to intercept the secret key in transit and then read, modify and forge the encrypted messages. One way around this is a private and public key encryption, where only the public key is used in transit but the message has to be decrypted by the private key, to which only the end user has access. However, this technology is still being developed.

Another proposed method of encryption is that of embedding serial copy protection in digital recordings, intended to prevent the making of more than one digital copy of those recordings. However, the embedded protection can easily be stripped out using widely available software. One of these methods may ultimately prove to be the way forward, but in the meantime the encryption debate rages on…

is encryption the answer?

SDMI isn't necessarily fighting a losing battle, but it does have an uphill struggle before it. Indeed, there's an argument that the industry doesn't need to worry about encryption at all.

When you reduce music to a series of 0s and 1s, you create such a free flow of information that no one secured mechanism or system is going to be able to prevent those who want to get around the prevention technology from finding a way of doing so. The emphasis should therefore shift to making access to downloadable music as simple and as user-friendly as possible, so that the vast majority of consumers will prefer to pay to receive music from a well-designed, easily identifiable web site operating a consumer-friendly after-sales service, with guarantees, exchange and refund policies and so on.

For the ordinary music enthusiast, the knowledge that his credit-card details and other personal data aren't going to be abused by the web-site operator, and the assurance that he'll receive exactly what he's paying for, should act as a real incentive not to pursue the alternative route of spending ages searching for pirate web sites and illegally downloading tracks for free.

Champions of the MP3 format – in particular Bob Kohn, chairman of the EMusic division of the EMusic/CDuctive corporation – are quick to point out what they perceive as a fallacy in the encryption arguments, using Microsoft as an example of a business that prospered *because* it eschewed a tightly controlled approach to the distribution of its software packages, rather than in spite of it. Microsoft figured that there would always be a small element of consumers pirating its software, but that this was preferable to spending billions of dollars and endless man-hours developing encryption technologies in the hope of protecting it.

It's a persuasive argument, but although the principle of making the product that you're selling more attractive to buy than pirate is a lesson that the record industry would do well to heed, it's also a disingenuous argument voiced by a company with a vested interest in the development of MP3 as the legitimate download format of choice. Music is easily divisible into tiny, three-minute packages, which makes it infinitely easier to pirate than a complex software package such as Microsoft Office, which is heavily reliant on after-sales service, back-up support and access to manuals for it to run successfully.

In consequence, music is a much easier target for pirates. Since Bob Kohn and his investors have spent millions of dollars on buying up rights in order to legitimately sell independent labels' catalogue online, only to see EMusic flounder in competition with Napster's unencrypted file-sharing service, he might now be tempted to review his argument. The bottom line is that the record industry needs either to focus on developing technologies which permit both a secure and speedy delivery of digital music or to find a way of harnessing Napster-style unencrypted technology and obtaining payment from its use.

Encryption technology alone isn't going to successfully combat piracy, at least not for the next few years. Robust and uniform copyright laws, working in harmony across the globe, are also going to have a part to play in deterring the pirates. However, adapting and updating copyright law to cope with the demands of the internet isn't a straightforward task.

copyright and music

Copyright is a tricky subject. Even lawyers find it difficult, and that's before you take into consideration the spin that the internet puts on it. Before exploiting music on the internet – whether this is selling physical copies of records, streaming music as an online radio station, downloading or webcasting – you'll need an understanding of how copyright works. In particular, you should appreciate how one piece of music can give rise to several different rights, requiring you to approach several different people for permission, depending on the use you wish to make of that particular piece of music.

what is copyright?

Let's begin by looking at the particular characteristics of copyright as it relates to music:

- Copyright is literally the right to prevent someone else from copying your original work;

- Copyright exists to protect creative works which would otherwise be vulnerable to unauthorised exploitation, such as music, art and literature;

- In order to be entitled to copyright protection, the creative work in question has to fall within a prescribed category of protected works. Musical works and sound recordings are both accorded protection, while lyrics are also protected as literary works;

- The work must be original (ie not copied) and, although its creation must have involved skill and labour, the work created does not have to achieve a minimum standard or quality in order to attract copyright (which is a pity, given the surfeit of late-'90s boy bands!);

- The work must be reduced to a material, or permanent, form in order to acquire protection – written down as sheet music, for example, or recorded onto a cassette. There is no copyright in an idea;

- There are two different copyrights subsisting in a recorded song (actually, three, if you count the lyrics): a copyright in the sound recording, which lasts for 50 years from the end of the year in which the recording was first recorded – or, if later, released – and a copyright in the underlying composition, which lasts for 70 years from the end of the year in which the composer died (or the last of the composers died, if there were more than one);

- To qualify for copyright protection, the copyright owner must be a "qualified person" (ie a citizen of or resident in the UK or one of the countries which are party to the Berne Convention or the Universal Copyright Convention);

- If a work is entitled to copyright protection, the copyright owner is able to prevent or restrict others from performing certain specified acts in relation to that work, which are known as the *restricted acts*;

- The restricted acts – or, put another way, the exclusive rights – given to the copyright owner are set out in the Copyright, Designs And Patents Act of 1988 (which will be referred to as the Copyright Act for short).

who is entitled to copyright protection?

Broadly speaking, the creator of the copyright work is the person entitled to copyright protection. The creator, or *first owner*, will differ depending on whether we're discussing the song or its recording.

Copyright In A Musical Work

The first owner of a musical work is the composer of the music and author of the lyrics. This may well be one and the same person. Alternatively, there may be joint authors of the music and/or the lyrics and/or both. A claimant to joint authorship must establish that he made a significant and original contribution to the creation of the work, and that he did so pursuant to a common design.

Copyright In A Recording

The author – and therefore the first owner – of a recording is the producer of the recording. The term "producer" is defined in the Copyright Act as "the person by whom the arrangements necessary for the making of the sound recording are undertaken". In practice, this will normally mean the person who pays for the recording, ie the record company. Because it can be argued that the "producer" of the sound recording is an individual, as the term is widely used and understood within the industry, the record company will ensure that any individuals who are involved with production enter into an agreement assigning all possible present and future copyright in the recording to the record company.

the song remains the same

Confused? There's no need to be. Copyright law can get a little dry, so now that you appreciate that one recording can give rise to different copyrights, usually owned by different people, let's take a closer look at how this fits together in practice by examining a real piece of music.

Take the track 'Kashmir' by Led Zeppelin, from the 1975 album *Physical Graffiti*. The music was written by Jimmy Page and, unusually, drummer John Bonham. (If you've heard the track, you'll know why Bonzo got a writing credit.) Page and Bonham therefore originally owned the copyright in the music. Robert Plant is also credited as a composer, because he wrote the lyrics. (Remember, a separate copyright exists in lyrics as a literary work.)

Since Page, Plant and Bonham were working together on 'Kashmir', pursuant to a common design, the law views them as joint authors of the composition. This basically means that they need each other's consent to decide whether 'Kashmir' should be used as the soundtrack to an advert for home furnishings, for example.

As original copyright owners, Page, Plant and Bonham assigned their interest in the song to their publishing company, MCA Music, who, as the new owners of the copyright in 'Kashmir', would be entitled to collect mechanical royalties, synchronisation fees (from the song's appearance in films, adverts, etc), the publisher's share of PRS and other performance income and sheet-music sales. (The meaning of each of these expressions is examined later.)

MCA would probably have kept 20-25% of the song's income as their commission and passed the rest to the writers. More recent CD versions of the album credit Flames Of Albion Music as the publisher – presumably the writers' own publishing company – after the expiration of the term of the MCA deal.

The copyright in the recording of 'Kashmir' is owned by Atlantic Records, who signed Led Zeppelin to an exclusive recording contract in 1969, funded the recording and arranged the studio time. Unlike the publishing contract, Atlantic will have owned the copyright outright from the inception of the recording, and will continue to own it for the life-span of copyright (50 years from the year of first release). Atlantic will collect income from record sales, public performance income from radio and TV plays and synchronisation fees for the use of the recorded rights. They will pay all of the members of Led Zeppelin a royalty for their performance on the recording, irrespective of who wrote the music, which is no concern of theirs – unless, of course, Zep had subtly incorporated the ideas of some old delta bluesman and clearance was required for their usage. (I notice that Willie Dixon is now credited as a co-writer of 'Whole Lotta Love'…)

so, where are we now?

To recap, Flames Of Albion Music now own the copyright in the musical work, after it was assigned to them by Page, Bonham and Plant, and Atlantic Records own the copyright in the recording.

The next thing to understand is that within the umbrella of those two main rights lurk several smaller, more specific rights that Flames Of Albion Music and Atlantic Records enjoy, as the present owners of the two main copyrights. Why a whole bundle of different rights? It's pretty logical, if you think about it. Recordings and compositions give rise to lots of different uses. I may want to start an internet radio station and broadcast your songs. You may want to play a live gig in which you perform your songs. Your record company will want to copy your song thousands of times over onto little plastic discs. Each right needs to be spelled out so that the owner of that particular right can be paid for it and control its use.

There are only a limited handful of such rights in existence (although the internet has given rise to a few new ones that no one had thought of before, as we'll see later in the chapter). Let's take each of these different rights in turn.

what rights do copyright owners enjoy?

The Copyright Act provides us with the following exhaustive list of individual rights. These are:

- The right to copy the work – in other words, to reproduce the work in any material form, for example by recording it onto disc (the *reproduction* right);

- The right to issue, or distribute, copies of the work to the public (the *distribution* right);

- The right to rent or lend copies of the work to the public (the *rental and lending* right);

- For compositions, the right to perform the work in public; and for recordings, the right to play or – if it is an audio-visual recording – show the work in public (the *public performance* right);

- The right to broadcast the work or to include the work in a cable programme service (the *broadcast* right and the *cable programme* right);

- For compositions, the right to make an adaptation of the work (the *adaptation* right).

clearing copyright for internet use

By now, it will be apparent that, before you're able to commercially exploit a piece of copyright music, you'll need to be clear about which rights you're intending to use, and you'll need to approach the relevant owner or holder of those rights. Going back to our previous example, let's assume that an internet radio station wanted to stream or webcast 'Kashmir' online and make it available as an exclusive download. Whose permission do they need, and what rights are they using?

Determining permission looks fairly easy. The current owners of the copyright in the music and the recording are Flames Of Albion Inc and Atlantic Records Limited, respectively. However, if you own *Physical Graffiti*, you'll also have noticed a credit appearing for ASCAP (the Association of Songwriters, Composers And Publishers), a US organisation responsible for granting blanket licences to radio stations, among other organisations, in order to allow them to play their members' work in public. (The UK equivalent is the PRS.) So, in order to digitally transmit the song, our friends at the internet radio station will also need blanket licences from ASCAP, the PRS, the equivalent societies in Japan, Germany and so on, because, as the internet is a global medium, who knows where the listeners will be? Right? Well, no, wrong actually. It would be pretty impractical to try and get licences from all around the world. A licence from the country in which the station is based should suffice – or, at least, it will do when the international collection societies put in place reciprocal arrangements for licensing the internet use of music. (In fact, this is already happening, as we'll see in the next chapter.) And, of course, that's if a public performance licence is even needed in the first place. Now, this is where things start to get very tricky…

which rights are you using?

It's the copyright lawyer's job to decide what's happening during the downloading and streaming processes and to isolate which of the traditional rights of exploitation are being exercised on the digital version of 'Kashmir' as it travels though the labyrinthine corridors of the internet.

Where does a broadcast end and a sale begin? The payment consequences could be significant. If the 'Kashmir' stream is seen as a broadcast, does it therefore attract a PRS/ASCAP-type performance fee? Or, because the digital information making up 'Kashmir' remains where it is – on a virtual server – is it a reproduction that occurs rather than a distribution, therefore giving rise to a mechanical royalty?

As yet, no one seems to be able to answer these questions, least of all the collection societies, who are trying to charge for licensing rights that they may or may not have. Therefore, the safest route is to obtain permission from every possible interested party before you start downloading music from the net. In the next chapter, we'll look at internet radio stations and run through all of the different people and organisations you'll need to approach in order to cover yourself.

So, what if you don't get permission from the various owners or administrators of these rights, and you go ahead anyway with an unauthorised download of 'Kashmir', for example? Can you be clobbered as a result? Before answering this question, there's a rumour that needs clearing up.

music on the internet – is it free?

This is an important question, because several million people don't seem to have grasped the answer yet, which is, of course, no – unless the artist, record company or whoever owns the rights to the track makes it freely available on the internet and want it to be free. It's their choice and theirs only. The misconception that music is somehow always available for free on the internet stems from two sources:

• The fact that there is no government authority controlling the internet;

• The wide availability of free MP3 music on the internet, legitimately or otherwise, which has created a culture of free music.

The copyright laws that we're looking at in this chapter apply to everyone who listens to music, as well as to content providers and those exploiting music for commercial gain. Copyright law also applies to music wherever and however it is disseminated, although with some difficulty insofar far as the internet is concerned, as illustrated below.

Copying a file, like copying a CD, is illegal, unless the copy is being used for private, study or review purposes only. It is irrelevant whether the file copied was obtained free of charge or was paid for. If a listener makes a copy of an MP3 file and distributes it among his friends, he is breaking the law.

All the same, many artists choose to give tracks away for free on the internet and will probably be quite happy for their fans to make copies of them and e-mail them to their friends – after all, it's great publicity for young, unknown artists – but take note that, in this case, each artist remains the owner of the copyright and can choose to enforce his rights at any time. If you're setting up an internet radio station and/or selling or downloading music over the net, you'll need various consents and licences in order to do so, as with the 'Kashmir' scenario above. If you fail to obtain them, you'll risk being held liable for infringing copyright.

how is copyright infringed?

In order to determine if a copyright owner's rights have been infringed, it is first necessary to show that any of the restricted acts have been performed in relation to "a substantial part of the work". The courts don't judge "substantial" purely in terms of quantity (although this may be a factor that they take into account) but instead primarily in terms of the importance or quality of the material infringed. It will be a question of fact in each case whether a copyright work has been infringed. For example, copying the distinctive two-bar guitar riff that opens 'Layla' will constitute infringement, even though the phrase lasts only a few seconds. In this case, the right infringed will be the reproduction right.

Even if substantial use has taken place in relation to a copyright work, it won't be an infringement if one of the exceptions to copyright infringement applies. The main exception is a *fair dealing* in relation to the work. A fair dealing encompasses research or private study, criticism or review and the reporting of current events.

Finally, having established that the act in question is one of the restricted acts – ie that a substantial part of the work has been infringed and that no possible exemption applies – the copyright owner must show that the person who has committed the alleged infringement "had access to and was aware of the original work". In other words, a causal connection must be made; copying – unconscious or otherwise – must be proved.

how is copyright protected?

As mentioned above, if you write the music and lyrics of a song, you are the first owner of the copyright in that song – there is no legal requirement to register the copyright. So how can you go about protecting it? (Take note that you can't prove that you own copyright, but you can establish the existence of a copyright from a specific date.)

- You can send a copy of the song to yourself – either in the form of sheet music or recorded onto a physical format, such as DAT or cassette – by registered post. When the envelope arrives, don't open it! Keep it safe, with the registered post receipt attached, clearly showing the date that it was sent. The unopened envelope will be admissible in court as evidence of your ownership.

- You can deposit a copy of the cassette or sheet music with your bank.

- You can ask a solicitor to sign and date the sheet music or cassette, and if necessary he will be able to swear an affidavit of his receipt at a later date.

copyright on the internet

why do we need new copyright laws?

The copyright laws that have been examined so far in this chapter provide songwriters, record companies and other rights holders with only limited protection against the unauthorised use of their music on the internet.

In the UK, the Copyright Act gives copyright owners the right to copy their work "in any material form, including storing the work in any medium by electronic means", while copying is also defined as including "transient copying". The use of the expressions "electronic means" and "transient copying" indicates that copyright owners have a limited ability to prevent unauthorised copying of their work on the internet.

But what of the other rights enjoyed by copyright owners? Do owners have the right to distribute, rent, lend, publicly perform or broadcast their works on the internet? No. UK law provides no protection for copyright owners in relation to the internet, other than the exclusive right to copy their work.

- The distribution right relates only to physical copies of the work and doesn't encompass digital deliveries of works.

- The rental and lending right is only relevant to renting or lending physical copies of the works.

- In English law, the right to perform works in public refers to a group of people physically gathered together at the same time. As internet transmissions take place on a one-to-one basis (except, perhaps, live webcasts), it's difficult to argue that a public performance of the work has taken place. How this squares with the view held by the PRS and ASCAP – that they should be entitled to collect and distribute public performance income – isn't entirely clear.

- The right to broadcast works means transmission by "wireless" means. Therefore, virtually all internet transmissions will be excluded.

As you can see, there is consequently a need for new legislation in order to address these issues and to ensure that record companies, publishers, writers and musicians get paid for and can control unauthorised exploitation of their work on the internet.

the music industry vs the ISPs and telecommunications companies

Seconds out, round one. In order to address the problems posed by the distribution of music on the internet, we now have the Directive On Copyright And Related Rights In The Information Society, to give it its full title, although here we'll continue to refer to it as the Copyright Directive. Together with its sister legislation in the United States, the Digital Millennium Copyright Act, the Copyright Directive is a significant development for the music industry in its search to provide a stable legal framework for the legitimate exploitation of music on the internet. However, the Directive isn't ideally worded for the music industry, as will become clear.

First, though, a little background. Record companies – as well as the telecommunications industry and the major ISPs – lobbied furiously to ensure that the Directive dealt satisfactorily with their concerns for exploiting copyright material on the internet. The telecoms and service providers, in particular, sought and obtained some concessions on the key issues of copying and liability. Even musicians got involved. (Well, when royalties are at stake…) A campaign staged by an alliance of rights holders and artists helped to convince the European Parliament to support a number of key amendments to the proposed Directive. Indeed, a petition on copyright championed by Jean-Michel Jarre has been signed by an impressive array of major artists, including The Corrs and Robbie Williams, several of whom were in Strasbourg on the eve of the vote to lobby MEPs.

a new reproduction right

The Directive gives musicians and other rights holders greater protection by introducing a new copying or reproduction right, which means that both copyright owners and related rights holders are granted an exclusive right to authorise or prohibit "direct or indirect, temporary or permanent reproduction by any means in any form, in whole or in part" of a copyright work (Article 2). This wording clearly encompasses internet usage, and has the effect of clarifying and harmonising the position for the whole of the EU. Under this Directive, all unauthorised digital copying of a piece of music will be unlawful throughout the EU.

exceptions to the reproduction right – temporary copying

According to the Directive, the word "temporary" can mean both "transient" and "incidental". This is actually pretty important, as it means that, if a piece of music is stored on an ISP's e-mail server, for example, even if only in transit between two PCs, the ISP will then be said to have made a temporary copy of that piece of music. As you can imagine, this could lead to a rather unpleasant outcome for AOL, AltaVista and all the other ISPs if that piece of music happened to be an illegally downloaded MP3 file. (Still, I don't imagine Warner will be rushing to sue AOL for copyright infringement!)

In order to avoid this particular scenario, Article 5 of the Directive provides for an obligatory exception to the reproduction right for temporary copies. Consequently, internet users and ISPs will be able to make transient and incidental copies of a musical work, for example, without infringing copyright, as long as the temporary copy:

• Forms part of a technological process; *and*

- Facilitates effective functioning of transmission systems; *and*

- Has no independent economic significance in itself.

In simple language, this means that certain technical acts of reproduction dictated by technology will be exempt if they have no separate economic significance in themselves. This "temporary copies" exemption meets the concerns of ISPs, since temporary copying – or *cache copying* – will have to take place as part of the function of the internet.

Cache Copies

The motivation behind the Article 5 exemption is the need to cater for the problem of cache copies (remember, these are temporary or incidental copies of data stored on computers during transmission via the internet). The European Commission argues that an obligatory exemption for temporary copies is essential in order for temporary acts of reproduction which are "dictated by technology" to take place.

The music industry would prefer to have temporary copying exempted only if the internet user has prior authorisation from the record company or publisher. However, the Commission has rejected this suggestion because it feels that such a provision might "significantly risk impeding the free movement of works and services" in member states, and would be largely unworkable in practice.

For the European music industry, Article 5 is, therefore, a big blow. The UK government, influenced by the pre-eminence of the UK record industry, believes that the Commission has bowed to the telecommunications companies and multi-nationals, who have consistently been in favour of liberating the use of the internet.

the problem with the temporary copies exemption

It's inevitable that the online distribution of music will involve the creation of temporary cache copies of files during the transmission process. It's not acceptable that ISPs should be brought to book if the creation of such copies is an inherent part of the technological working of the internet. Provided that they are unaware that the material in transit has been illegally uploaded and/or is in the process of being illegally downloaded, the law should protect them.

It's also reasonable for rights holders to expect only authorised copies of their work to be transmitted on the internet. However, if they can't trace the infringers responsible for the unlawful transmission of their work (Freenet users, for example), they should be able to pursue the ISP directly if the ISP has been instrumental in the acts of piracy.

So, for ISPs the issue is one of liability – should they be held liable for copyright infringement in the event that unlawful material is being disseminated across their networks? The answer is, of course, no, provided that they're unaware of, or ought not to have known of, such unlawful material. And this is precisely the defence accorded to ISPs by the E-Commerce Directive, which of course begs the question, in that case, why is the temporary copies exemption needed in the Copyright Directive?

The temporary copies exemption can only hinder the fight against piracy, as well as erode the perceived value of music copyright in the online environment, particularly when seen in conjunction with the private copies exemption (see below), which is wide open to abuse. By creating a *carte blanche* temporary copies exemption, the law is serving only to create a disincentive for ISPs to dissuade them from co-operating with rights holders in pursuing the pirates. After all, why should they waste time and money in doing so if their own position is unassailable, regardless of their role in the infringement?

exceptions to the reproduction right – private copying

Article 5 of the Directive also provides for an *optional* exemption to the reproduction right for copying for private use. (Optional in this case means that different member states in the EU can choose whether or not to adopt this part of the Directive.) A distinction is made between analogue and digital copying. The record industry is worried that pirates could be encouraged by the existence of such an exemption. Insofar as digital copying is concerned, any exemption is wide open to abuse, so digital private copying will only be allowed if:

- It is for strictly personal and private use;

- It is for a non-commercial end;

- There are no reliable and effective technical means of protecting the interests of rights holders.

A Digital-Blank-Tape Levy

A right to fair compensation must be provided for all digital copying.

Effectively, this would entail the UK imposing some form of levy system on the purchase of recordable disks, digital audio tape and other recording materials. Four hundred artists signed a petition in support of this proposal to ensure that it was adopted by the European Parliament, but the UK government is unlikely to adopt such an idea. It's hard to calculate what "fair compensation" would mean, and how much of the compulsory levy would eventually trickle back to artists and other rights holders.

the problem with the private copies exemption

The private copies exemption represents a real problem in an online environment. For example, what if a global contingent of Radiohead fans decide to systematically download the new album from the internet, each individual justifying their actions by claiming that the resulting copy was for their private use only? In this case, millions of private copies of the album would have been legitimately downloaded without any payment to the artist or their record label. Such an action could severely damage the legitimate licensing of music.

a new right of communication to the public

Article 3 of the Directive introduces a newly-created right specifically to cater for the internet and new media. It is effectively the digital-distribution equivalent of physically distributing records. The right gives songwriters and publishers "the exclusive right to authorise or provide any communication to the public of originals and copies of their works, including the making available to the public of their works in such a way that members of the public may access them from a place and at a time individually chosen by them".

security and rights management

This part of the Copyright Directive is concerned with security and protection for rights holders in the Digital Age. Member states must now "provide adequate legal protection against the circumvention without authority of any effective technological measures designed to protect any copyright or related right". In plain English, you could face prosecution if, for example, you tried to get around an encryption system in order to bootleg music files. To be liable under these provisions, you must know, or have reasonable grounds for believing, that you are pursuing such an objective.

Member states also have to "provide adequate legal protection against any activities, including the manufacture or distribution of devices or the provision of services which are promoted or advertised for the purpose of circumvention". This means that you could face prosecution if you make or advertise equipment or, for example, run search engines that enable people to pirate music. Were the action against Napster to have been brought in the EU, and after the Copyright Directive had come into force, it's likely that it would have been alleged that Napster had breached this part of the Directive. Indeed, these provisions mirror those contained in recent US legislation. Speaking of which…

online copyright in the US

The US is the world's biggest territory for music sales and inevitably leads the field in the internet revolution of the music industry, so let's take a quick look at the way our transatlantic cousins are handling things.

In the US, streaming and webcasting are the current talking points for artists and rights holders seeking to obtain online copyright royalties. The US Copyright Office wants to effectively impose a mechanical royalty for streamed and webcast online radio. (This is something of a break with tradition, as until now radio stations have only paid composers performing rights royalties, as in the UK.) If the Copyright Office gets its way, online radio stations will have to pay mechanical royalties for a single performance of a song as well as performing royalties (ie those collected by ASCAP and the BMI).

The US has created a new term, "digital phonorecord deliveries", to describe the digital delivery of recordings on the internet. Not surprisingly, internet radio stations and webcasters, such as RealNetworks, argue that the streaming of digital phonorecord deliveries should make them exempt from liability for paying mechanical royalties. Does this argument sound familiar?

There is also the question of public performance royalties for the digital transmission of records. Historically, sound recordings were the only US copyright work denied the right of public performance. As we'll see in the following chapter, however, with the advent of two new pieces of legislation – the 1995 Digital Performance Right And Sound Recordings Act and the 1998 Digital Millennium Copyright Act – this has all changed.

internet DJs and internet radio

internet radio

One of the main growth areas in internet music exploitation is internet radio. Content providers and aggregators are excited about its potential for attracting users and pulling in advertising revenue. "The future has no frequency," as Storm Radio (http://www.stormlive.com) puts it. You don't tune into a signal; you just go to the appropriate web site and then you can take your chosen radio station with you while you surf the rest of the net. Internet radio is about putting out music around the clock, seven days a week, to any net user who cares to listen.

the future – online or digital?

There's a lot of speculation concerning the significance of internet radio. Listener figures are still very low, and there remains the possibility that eventually digital radio (the radio version of digital television stations, such as OnDigital) will displace its online competitor. There also remain uncertainties concerning how listener numbers will be measured. If it's impossible to measure audience figures, advertisers are unlikely to commit themselves to internet radio, and online stations could find themselves struggling through lack of funding.

Nonetheless, internet radio offers a cost-effective method of broadcasting content to a wide audience, and provides broadcasters with the opportunity to reach new types of listeners, particularly those in niche markets. This isn't the case with digital radio, which will be in competition with existing analogue broadcasters. Internet radio also has one major advantage over digital: cost. The internet radio stations are free for anyone with internet access, while digital radio involves buying a stand-alone device costing hundreds of pounds.

For now, digital and internet radio are both still in their embryonic stages. It remains to be seen whether the competing platforms can successfully co-exist, or whether one will ultimately dominate.

narrowcasting

Whether the future is online or digital, the real interest in current internet radio lies in its adoption of narrowcasting principles. Earlier, we looked at the internet's suitability for promoting niche music and for encouraging micro-markets. Nowhere is this better seen than in the development of internet radio. Online radio stations specialise in the genre-based approach, which means that you can choose the station that's dedicated to your taste in music – reggae, jungle, rock, hip-hop, etc. The mainstream commercial stations have also been quick to pick up on this; Capital's online division recently set up three new web-based stations, each catering for a very specific audience – Rage for the male PlayStation generation, Diva for working women and Urban Groove for the hip young soul/swingbeat crowd.

You just can't get this level of audience targeting on commercial airborne radio or on the BBC (with a few exceptions). The reason? Current regulation is totally opposed to narrowcasting. The Radio Communications Authority would never license a station to broadcast, say, heavy rock 24 hours a day. Indeed, the way in which Radio 1 has been heading in the last couple of years – with daytime radio playing almost exclusively next week's Top 20 and with A-list tracks (the Robbie Williams, All Saints and Madonnas of this world) earning up to 40 spins a week – there's virtually no room at all for specialist programming. If you aren't going to win a licence from the RCA to broadcast genre-based music, internet radio is really the only serious alternative.

Because of this, there's clearly a market for genre-based internet radio, just as there's a market for airborne genre-based radio – a market catered for by the pirates. The key is to offer web users exactly the right soundtrack to their net-surfing. If they trust that your station is always going to be playing their kind of music, and they can listen for free because they're surfing or e-mailing friends anyway, then you've got the right ingredients for building a listening base.

US internet radio – music on demand

In the US, internet radio is already well established, with an average of around four million listeners per week, and this is due in no small part to the fact that most web users in the States get free, unmetered access to the net. Internet radio is also a logical step on from college radio, which has always concentrated on adopting a specialist approach to music.

Taking the lead from developments Stateside, the next step from narrowcasting will, in all likelihood, be music on demand, or interactive radio. Online music providers will allow users to create their own custom online radio stations by enabling them to choose a genre and then determine their preferences, so that only music from artists they like will be played – the ultimate dream playlist. Again, this fits neatly with the current trend in music exploitation on the internet that has been highlighted throughout the book – the establishment of a subscription-based model, by which listeners can choose the music they want to listen to, download or stream from a few powerful content aggregators.

However, there are a few restrictions in US that must be observed when operating a music-on-demand radio station, which we'll look at in the section on the Digital Millennium Copyright Act later in this chapter.

what do you need?

Setting up an internet radio station is pretty straightforward. The RCA's laws don't apply to online broadcasters, so you don't need a broadcasting licence. Nor does a computer-based online network need an expensive transmitter to power broadcasts. In fact, probably the most complicated aspect of running an internet radio station is making sure that you've cleared all of the necessary rights that will enable you to do so legitimately.

how do you go about clearing rights?

Clearing rights for internet radio use is a time-consuming business. The law is currently in a state of flux and it's not entirely certain which rights need to be cleared, so you should play it safe and cover every possibility. You'll need to clear rights from a variety of sources, for every conceivable use that you may wish to make of a piece of music on the internet. So, using first a UK-based music provider and then a US-based online station as our examples, let's find our way through the maze. Our first port of call is the collection societies.

royalty collection societies

The UK's main royalty collection societies are the PPL and the PRS/MCPS Music Alliance.

- The PPL (Phonographic Performance Limited) licenses the public performance of recordings.

- The PRS (Performing Right Society) licenses the public performance of songs.

- The MCPS (Mechanical Copyright Protection Society) licenses the reproduction of songs on records.

We'll take a more detailed look at each later, but for now it's enough to know that they all have an important role to play in ensuring that musicians and other rights holders get paid for the exploitation of their music on the internet. The collection societies have two main tasks: to identify rights usage and to police and track the use of music online. However, as with virtually every aspect of the music industry, the collection societies are struggling to keep up with the pace of change brought about by the internet, and they really need to catch up because arguably they're more important now than ever before. There are literally thousands of new radio stations and webcasters of all shapes and sizes broadcasting online, and very few of them are paying copyright owners for the privilege.

clearing rights in the UK

streaming – clearing rights in recordings

The PPL

The streaming or webcasting of master recordings online will amount to a public performance or broadcast of those recordings, and permission will need to be sought from the copyright owners of the recordings to allow clips or whole tracks to be streamed.

As yet, the PPL – who represent over 2,000 record companies, both majors and independents – are unable to grant blanket licences on behalf of their members for the online licensing of recordings, as the record companies, wary of the growing importance of online distribution, haven't yet agreed to assign the necessary rights to the PPL that would enable it to license internet use. This means that online radio stations and other webcasters will have to go through the hoops and approach each individual record company in order to clear the use of the copyright in the sound recordings that they wish to use.

The PPL *are* able to license the use of sound recordings in all forms of radio and television, including terrestrial, satellite or cable – both digital and analogue – and internet simulcasts of UK radio broadcasts. However, internet simulcasts cover only the situation in which a normal terrestrial radio station is also broadcasting simultaneously over the internet.

There is a danger that the PPL might find itself in an increasingly marginalised position as online licensing becomes ever more significant. The current situation bears interesting similarities to a process which is beginning to take hold in the US: source licensing. In recent years, the powerful US broadcast and cable networks have been lobbying congress for the right to bypass the collection societies (ASCAP and the BMI) altogether. The idea is that, by negotiating with individual labels *at source*, the broadcasters will be able to beat them down over price rather than face the heavy negotiating power of a collection society which owns the right to license thousands of songs. The broadcasters believe that this idea will be attractive to record companies, because they'll be able to cut out the collection societies' administration fees. Source licensing isn't legal yet, but the possibility of it happening should be enough to keep the collection societies on their toes.

In the meantime, though, are there any ways around the PPL problem? Well, the PPL are no longer the only significant UK body in a position to grant blanket licences for sound recordings. In the past couple of years, a new and forward-thinking trade body has sprung into existence: AIM.

AIM

"We want our music to be accessible to anyone who wants to use it, but the independent sector is the hardest for new media to deal with, as we are the most fragmented."
  – Martin Mills, MD, Beggars Banquet

AIM, the Association of Independent Music, is an increasingly powerful organisation, representing some 400 independent record companies in the UK – including XL, Beggars Banquet, V2, Mute, Ministry Of Sound and Telstar – and around a quarter of the UK's retail sector. AIM promotes the use of its members' music and protects their interests in the recorded music market.

AIM have stolen a march on the PPL in setting up a trial online scheme (note: for UK use only), based on six-monthly investigations into internet radio and prevailing methods of charging. It's all very *ad hoc* at the moment, and can really only be seen, at best, as an interim solution.

The current arrangement means that you'll be able to negotiate a trial "licence" with AIM enabling you to use all of AIM members' catalogue (unless a particular label decides to opt out) in return for paying AIM a variable administration fee. Okay, so the playlists will have to consist solely of AIM members' recordings, but that's still a pretty vast and eclectic repertoire from which to choose, including Prodigy, Moby, Stereophonics, Travis, etc. Indeed, several internet broadcasters have already negotiated licences with AIM in this way, including NME, Carlton Interactive, Capital and Storm.

Dealing Directly With The Majors

In addition to obtaining an AIM licence, you'll also have the option of augmenting your playlist by negotiating with individual labels. Given that Warner, EMI, BMG, Sony and Universal own several thousand copyrights between them, this isn't as unrealistic a suggestion as it might otherwise seem. If you have the time and resources available, the sensible approach would be to negotiate royalty payments and to clear rights in advance of launching the station, as Chrysalis New Media did with their Ride The Tiger music and lifestyle venture, which went online at the tail end of 2000.

streaming – clearing performing rights (PRS licences)

UK law currently views web sites as being analogous to cable programme services (the *Shetland Times* case). In the UK, the rights to perform, broadcast and include a musical work in a cable programme service are controlled by the Performing Right Society (PRS) on behalf of its members.

The PRS administers licences for the online use of musical works on this basis, describing the process as "licensing the presentation of music on a web site". The PRS grants various forms of blanket licence, with tariffs varying depending on the use made of the licensed music on the site. For example, a restricted use of, say, 30-second clips would probably fall into the minimum charge schedule of £1.37 per day. At the other end of the spectrum, a major music organisation with a significant repertoire may pay the equivalent of £27.40 per day.

The PRS has now entered into a series of reciprocal, bilateral agreements with other major collection societies, including BMI (the USA), BUMA (Holland), GEMA (Germany) and SACEM (France). Other societies – including ASCAP – are expected to sign up shortly.

So, if you're a music provider wishing to stream or webcast internet radio in, say, the UK, the US, France and Germany, which collection society should you approach in order to obtain a licence – bearing in mind that you'll now only need one? The licence will be issued by the local collecting society in the country of *economic residence* of the owner of the web site – and the fees applicable will be those of the local collecting society.

downloading – clearing mechanical rights

Ostensibly, you'll need to approach the publisher or the writer (if the writer is self-published) for the use of the copyright in the musical work, if you intend to make downloads available from your site. If your online radio station is only using streamed audio, it's debatable (but not certain) whether a mechanical licence is required at all (the so-called "ephemeral" copies exemption – see the US section of this chapter for more information). Fortunately, there is an alternative to approaching each individual publisher/writer – you can obtain a blanket licence from the MCPS half of the PRS/MCPS Music Alliance on behalf of all of its members in the UK.

The mechanical right is the song composer's and the publisher's main source of income. Each time a song is incorporated on a record, it gives rise to a payment of a mechanical royalty. It's known as a *mechanical* right because the term was originally coined to refer to the song being mechanically reproduced on vinyl. The MCPS's involvement in the alliance's proposed licensing regime for online radio is therefore controversial, to say the least. Despite the fact that music online has no physical form, the MCPS have successfully argued that its distribution involves a mechanical reproduction. This argument seems to have taken root in the US, too.

The MCPS grant blanket licences of what they refer to as "repertoire works" on behalf of their members (ie composers and publishers), and anyone wishing to download music from their web site needs to approach the MCPS and apply for a licence. As yet, the MCPS doesn't have a full licensing scheme in place for the online supply of music, but it is currently granting licences on an interim basis.

The basis upon which MCPS grants licences is as follows:

• Downloads to members of the public in the UK – 10p per musical work per UK download for each musical work of up to five minutes in duration and an additional 2p per minute thereafter for each download of any work exceeding five minutes;

- Downloads to members of the public outside the UK. The published applicable local royalty rates will apply. In the absence of a published local rate, the UK rate will apply.

Record-industry bodies the BPI and AIM are still in negotiation with the MCPS over the proposed download rate of 10p per track, and have yet to agree to it. This is more than record companies have traditionally paid, and they fear that it will prohibit the development of music on the internet.

Online music providers will be obliged to account to the MCPS on a quarterly basis, listing all repertoire works downloaded in the previous quarter and the territory in which each download took place. The current licensing scheme is applicable for permanent downloads and also allows the service provider to stream audio clips up to a maximum of 30 seconds for free, while any audio clip in excess of 30 seconds will incur a licence fee. One option would be to download in a non-permanent form, ie one where the download expires after a prescribed period of time – 28 days, for example. This would still mean that the content provider would have to obtain a licence from the MCPS, but this would be on a different basis to that of the permanent download licence, and presumably cheaper.

When obtaining a licence from the MCPS for the online supply of music, the provider must undertake that it will comply with the security standards defined in the SDMI phase one specification for portable devices and other relevant SDMI specifications.

general – clearing synchronisation rights

The synchronisation right is the right to use music in timed synchronisation with visual images, for example on a film soundtrack, in a TV advert or in a promo video. A synchronisation licence – or *synch licence*, as it's commonly known – will also be needed where a musical work is incorporated into a multimedia product, such as a streamed audio-visual clip or a live concert webcast marrying images and sound. This right to synchronise the music will be held by the publisher or composer; collection societies don't have the authority to grant blanket synchronisation licences in any medium, the exception being music videos, the rights in which will be administered by VPL (Video Performance Ltd) in the UK.

clearing rights in the US

streaming – clearing rights in recordings

Until the passing of the Digital Performance Right And Sound Recordings Act (or Digital Performance Act, for short) in 1995, artists and record companies in the US had never been entitled to receive performance income for the public performance of master recordings, which is unlike the position in the rest of the world. In the UK, for example, record companies and artists are entitled to an equal split of PPL income arising from the performance of recordings. The US, however, has no PPL equivalent.

The Digital Performance Act changed this position, insofar as recordings are streamed or webcast online (although there is still no entitlement to performance income for records played on the radio, television and in cinemas, etc). Internet radio stations will have to clear rights and pay performance royalties for the digital radio transmission of audio-only records.

The digital performance right is therefore very limited, or at least it was until the passing of the Digital Millennium Copyright Act (see later). However, if you're intending to stream music via a subscription-based service, you'll need to obtain a licence to do so. And how do you go about getting a licence? Well, the answer to this question depends on whether or not you're entitled to qualify for a compulsory licence. Under the Digital Performance Act, there are two main criteria that an internet broadcaster will need to meet:

- You'll have to be operating a streaming rather than a download-based service;

- The transmission must not be interactive or "on demand".

As long as these criteria are met, you will then be entitled to a compulsory licence from the owner of the rights in the recordings, in return for paying the statutory fee. (In practice, the RIAA will issue statutory licences on behalf of the copyright owners.) Digital broadcasts of audio-only records that don't fall within the above categories, or the new categories created by the Digital Mechanical Copyright Act (DMCA), are subject to voluntary licensing and a negotiated fee. As there is no organisation authorised to grant licences on behalf of copyright owners to webcasters that don't qualify for the statutory licence, each copyright owner must be contacted individually.

You will be aware, by now, that a licence to *perform* a recording isn't the only licence required by an online radio webcaster. It is, of course, inevitable that a *copy* of each sound recording will be made in the webcaster's server prior to transmission of that recording. As the law views these as "ephemeral" recordings, there is no need for the webcaster to obtain a separate licence to reproduce the recordings (provided, of course, that no more than one ephemeral copy is produced and that no downloading is taking place, and provided that certain other strict criteria – as laid down in the DMCA – are met).

clearing performing rights in compositions

In the US, as in the UK, the performing rights of songwriters have always been safeguarded, although in the US by the BMI and ASCAP (the US equivalents of the PRS). As in the UK, ASCAP and the BMI have asserted their right to license performing rights for online exploitation.

US law views each internet transmission of a musical work as a public performance of that work. The ASCAP licence authorises online broadcasters to perform any and all of the individual musical works in ASCAP's repertoire by means of web site transmissions. This authorisation extends to all such performances regardless of the file formats in which the transmissions take place.

ASCAP offers three different rate schedules to accommodate different levels of music use, and at the time of writing the minimum fee payable under the ASCAP licensing agreement is $264 per year. In order to obtain the licence, owners of online radio stations should visit http://www.ascap.com and download the "ASCAP Licence Agreement For Internet Sites On The Worldwide Web". The licence fee is payable on a quarterly basis either on or before the usual quarter days. For BMI repertoire, note the BMI's involvement in the series of bilateral agreements entered into with the PRS, GEMA, BUMA and SACEM (see above).

downloading – clearing mechanical rights

The copying of a copyrighted musical work onto an online radio broadcaster's server (other than a one-off ephemeral copy, as explained above) constitutes exploitation and/or distribution of the reproduction right, for which authorisation from the Harry Fox Agency (the US equivalent of the MCPS) is required. The Digital Performance Act requires that a compulsory mechanical licence must be obtained for the right to distribute (ie download) recordings by means of digital transmission (in exchange for paying the statutory fee of $0.075 per song up to five minutes in length).

the Digital Millennium Copyright Act

The Digital Millennium Copyright Act, passed in 1998, extended the digital transmission right introduced by the Digital Performance Act to cover cable and satellite digital audio services, webcasts and all future forms of digital transmission of audio-only records. Most non-interactive transmissions are now therefore subject to statutory licensing at rates to be negotiated or, if necessary, arbitrated. However, traditional radio and television broadcasts remain exempt from these provisions.

The DMCA also contains several important provisions which have the effect of mirroring the Copyright and E-Commerce Directives rolled into one. As such, it encompasses the following:

- The Act seeks to prohibit the manufacture and distribution of software and hardware used to undermine electronic "locks" or otherwise designed with the express purpose of circumventing encryption devices or codes, such as software capable of converting encrypted Liquid Audio files into .WAV files;

- The Act outlines the responsibilities of ISPs in guarding against online piracy. In this regard, the law formalises a notice and "takedown" procedure between ISPs and copyright owners. The Act also provides for a so-called "safe-harbour", shielding ISPs from liability for any infringing and/or illegal material uploaded onto their servers. It's now clear that, when an ISP is aware that it's posting or transmitting infringing content, it must act to remove the infringing works or it may be liable for any resulting damages;

- The Act also addresses the rights of copyright owners and other rights holders, together with detailing provisions for the licensing of music online.

DJs and the internet

supplying your services on the net

As internet radio stations and interactive/streamed on-demand broadcasting proliferates, top-name DJs who can bring that touch of "street" and cutting-edge cool craved by white middle-class businessmen running web sites for white middle-class investors are becoming hot property.

Web-based radio stations, such as Hedd.net and Trust The DJ, as well as major broadcasters, such as the BBC, are keen to sign up top-name DJs to endorse their sites, broadcast shows, perform exclusive mixes and recommend records for them to sell to the kids. Mainly aimed at the hip-hop, R&B and dance scene, most of these sites are, at present, a sort of hybrid of *Mixmag* and Kiss FM. They need to develop a stronger identity and bring something a little newer to the party – maybe make more of the interactive elements of the internet that will allow their listeners to perform live mixes of tracks "on air". Nonetheless, they represent a useful money-spinner for DJs, allowing them to bring their typical club sets into people's living rooms via their PCs.

As always, however, there are a few things to look out for when doing a deal like this, so let's run through the problem areas.

exclusivity

As a successful DJ, you will probably already be contracted through a record label or two to produce DJ/mix compilation albums. These albums, and any future releases on other labels, must be excluded from your internet agreement. This is a mainstay of your income, and any label to whom you grant your DJing rights will want to exploit the recordings in all formats and all media, including the internet, and unless you make it clear in the agreement that you are excluding specific deals from your obligation to provide exclusive services, you won't be able to prevent them from doing so.

clearing rights

Ensure that it is the online radio provider's responsibility to clear the usage of any of the recordings or musical works that you recommend. This is something of a nightmare, as we've already seen throughout this chapter.

endorsement services

You will be forbidden from providing endorsement services to or for any other third party. This is okay, provided that the third party is specifically a web-based competitor of your internet radio station. Obviously, this provision can't also include terrestrial, satellite or other non-internet broadcasters.

your obligations

Some online radio providers will ask you not to grant any licence or permit any recording that you produce during the term to be distributed by or on behalf of any third party via digital or online media. As I mentioned earlier, any deal that you strike with Sony, Ministry Of Sound or any other company will inevitably involve the granting of digital rights, and you won't be able to prevent this. In consequence, such a clause must be deleted from the agreement.

links to other web sites

Once you're contracted to an online radio provider, they will effectively be hosting your official presence on the net. As a result, there have to be several obligations imposed upon the provider, including a guarantee that they will provide a link to a third-party web site providing fulfilment of, or a portal for, merchandising sales and ticket sales. This is particularly important if the provider isn't yet in a position to provide these services itself.

The online radio provider should be obliged to keep the web site updated at regular intervals and should be committed to spending a certain amount of money on ensuring that the site looks and feels good. You should, of course, have approval over this.

royalties and advances

Your advance should be payable on each anniversary of the agreement, and should ideally be set up as a "rolling" advance. (See Chapter 9).

Your royalty should be expressed as a percentage of the actual price achieved on the sale of any recommended tracks or records, net only of any sales taxes actually paid by the online radio provider. It is possible that they will locate the server outside the UK so that sales taxes aren't incurred.

One of your obligations may well be to recommend records by up-and-coming artists (for example, white labels and promos that find their way into the clubs before the labels come on board). If the online radio provider sells these records, via downloads or e-commerce sales, you should be entitled to a royalty or commission. Don't commit to receiving a royalty based on a price fixed in advance; as far as the price for any recommended products and services is concerned, this should be agreed from time to time as and when the recommended products and services are themselves agreed – again, don't tie yourself down. In addition, you should also be entitled to receive a percentage of any other income generated by the web site, however it arises – for example, in relation to streaming. You should also ask for the usual audit rights and for accounting to take place on a quarterly basis.

term

You shouldn't commit yourself to more than a maximum of three years from the date of signature, regardless of how long it takes for the online radio provider to get their site up and running. If they aren't online within, say, three months of signature, you should be able to automatically terminate the agreement.

A-list DJs

If you're a really big-name DJ, ie a Gilles Peterson or a Seb Fontaine, you should also be able to automatically terminate your internet agreement if at any one time there are less than, say, 15 "A-list" DJs exclusively signed to your online radio provider. You should attach a list of these DJs as a schedule to the agreement so that there's no dispute over the meaning of the term "A-List".

One final point: at the end of the term, all rights in the web site should revert to you.

mixing online

Several web sites have taken advantage of the internet's interactive capabilities by introducing online mixing facilities for budding DJs to hone their skills. These facilities can take the form of segueing tracks in twin-turntable style, adding scratches for that authentic vinyl sample effect and virtual mixing desks, where the levels and balances on different instruments can be adjusted by moving faders and EQs and experimenting with various outboard effects – reverb, delay, compression and so on. Try visiting http://www.onlinedj.com, http://www.turntable.de, http://www.ejay.com and http://www.getoutthere.com.

live music promoters and the internet

The internet isn't just opening up new opportunities for DJ's and online radio broadcasters; webcast technology played a significant role in reinvigorating the UK festival scene in 2000, and will continue to expand festival and live music revenues as broadband access becomes commonplace. All of the major festivals (including Glastonbury, Homelands, T In The Park, Lost Weekend, Creamfields and V2000) were webcast online last year by a variety of companies, including BBC Choice, NME, DV4 and Done And Dusted. In particular, webcasts:

- Increase broadcasting capacity to international audiences;

- Are an excellent way of providing festival-goers with information about line-ups, ticketing and so on in advance, and of disseminating this information quickly (Creamfields reached half a million people with their e-flyer in 2000);

- Offer great interactive opportunities, such as allowing the home audience to choose their own camera angles and to pick which artist and which stage they wish to see at any given time.

Organisations that specialise in organising live music events – festivals, gigs and so on – should also be alive to the marketing and promotional possibilities that webcasters and other internet companies can bring. If you're running an event the size of Glastonbury and can afford to live without major corporate sponsorship on political/credibility grounds, then that's all well and good. More realistically, with artists' fees spiralling ever upwards, commercial sponsorship deals can offer a vital financial contribution to the costs of running a live event. Nonetheless, the branding should still sit well with the festival's identity, and should be sensitive to artists' image. Nowadays, online sponsorship deals go way beyond the inclusion of simple banners and pop-up ads; the name of your sponsor will be splashed around the festival site on posters, stages, stalls, programmes and other festival paraphernalia.

One of the best types of deal for a live concert promoter is to find a specialist webcasting company who wants to cover the event. (Remember, we looked earlier at the popularity of live music events in driving traffic to a site.) You should be able to strike a mutually beneficial deal for all parties involved, in which the webcaster gets exclusive rights to show the event and to use the footage later (see below), the artists appearing gain extra exposure and you win sponsorship for the event, together with additional online promotion and access to professionally shot footage. So how do these deals work?

webcasting events – the agreement

The basis of a webcasting agreement will usually depend on the kind of event being covered. More often than not, however, the webcaster will be looking to sponsor the event that they will be broadcasting, and they will probably wish the sponsorship to be exclusive. However, you should limit the exclusivity to online sponsorship since you'll probably be lining up several other sponsors, particularly for a larger event such as a festival. Sponsoring will entail a raft of provisions entitling the webcaster to place their logo on all event publicity, to set up a joint web site with details of the event and to have their name generally plastered all over the venue. This is fair enough, since the webcasting company will be paying for the webcast and providing their equipment (on-location ISDN lines, live encoder, mixer, digital video desk and cameras and so on) and technical expertise.

webcasting agreements – areas to look for

Here are a few specific areas to be aware of in negotiating these agreements:

- The webcaster will probably ask for the right to license footage to third-party web sites and broadcasters. This should be made conditional upon obtaining your approval and upon the webcaster paying you an appropriate share of any income from such a rebroadcast;

- You may well be asked to obtain written confirmation from the artists performing at your event that they are happy for the webcaster to film, webcast and archive their set. Again, this is okay, but you should limit this by specifying that an artist's performance can only be webcast on a maximum of two occasions, that the webcast will be streamed only, that no downloading rights are granted and that the archive can only be used with the artist's approval;

- How much are you being paid? Apart from negotiating an advance, you will want to receive a percentage of the income derived from the webcasts. This should either be gross income or, if net income, the deductions should be specified. There should also be a clause in the contract obliging the webcaster to pay your share of the money within a few days of his receipt of the income, and you should have the usual audit rights;

- Clarify that the cost of providing the technical production equipment listed in the contract will be borne by the webcaster, and that they will be responsible for paying for any multimedia facilities, internet access, screens and so on;

- Can you use the webcast footage? It may be that there will be some stills that can be used for promo material or footage that you can use for your own videos;

- Ensure that you can terminate the agreement (and that the rights in the webcast revert to you) if the webcaster is in breach – for example, if they fail to pay or account to you or provide the technical expertise which they are contracted to supply;

- Clarify that the webcaster cannot assign the agreement, and that, if they wish to license it to a third party, you should receive a copy of the details of the licence, right of approval of the commercial terms, the identity of the licensee and, if possible, direct accounting;

- Ask for artistic and editorial control over the footage – you'll need to have approval over the final edit before it's webcast, unless it's going out live.

music equipment and the internet

MP3 players

The MP3 players covered here are virtual players, in that they have no physical presence in the same way as a CD player or a portable player, such as Diamond Multimedia's Rio, which play back MP3 files that have already been downloaded to your computer. In order to play these files in the first place, you have to install an MP3 player onto your hard drive.

Your choice of player won't be based on the question of cost – as with virtually any software on the net, you can get it for free or for a minimal sum. Be guided instead by the kinds of things that would inform your purchase of any home hi-fi equipment: sound, facilities, look, user-friendliness.

There are many MP3 players to choose from. A visit to a specialist software archive site, such as http://www.download.com or http://www.tucows.com, will make this immediately apparent. At either of these sites, if you key in "MP3" and specify the type of computer you're using, you'll be given a detailed description of every program that's available. Alternatively, you could read the next couple of pages and save yourself a lot of time and effort. Below are listed the most influential, most reviewed and, by some distance, most popular MP3 players currently on the market.

Winamp (http://www.winamp.com)

The most popular MP3 player is Winamp, or Windows Amplifier, the Mac-compatible version of which can be found at http://www.macamp.org. Winamp allows you to create a jukebox of MP3 files which you've already downloaded from the internet or that you've created yourself. Winamp's popularity rests in its slavish attention to detail and its near-flawless replication of the real thing. It features a ten-band graphic equaliser allowing you to choose or set the frequencies of the track you're listening to. Once selected, your chosen frequency settings can then be saved and automatically loaded the next time you play that track. The more retentive users (probably males who delight in sending each other compilation tapes of obscure tracks) will doubtless take great pleasure in the facilities available, which will allow them to record all of the track data, including song titles and timings, genre and even mood. The Playlist feature allows you to add and remove files, sort list by title, by filename and so on to create your own custom playlist of songs.

One of the biggest reasons for Winamp's popularity is its ability to shed its "skin" in favour of a different visual cover. This enables you to choose the look of your player without altering its functionality. There are literally hundreds of different skins available for free at the Winamp and Macamp web sites.

Sonique (http://www.sonique.com)

Where Winamp is very much a virtual reproduction of a traditional amplifier, it's immediately clear that Sonique has much more of the look and feel of a Digital-Age amplifier. It is also arguably a better-sounding player.

At the core of Sonique is its 20-band graphic equaliser, which gives users a smooth waveform to adjust rather than numerous EQ sliders. Anyone used to chopping up samples will find this a familiar way of representing sound frequencies.

However, editing and re-ordering your songs in the playlist isn't as user-friendly as it is with Winamp. On the positive side, however, it contains a built-in web search facility, allowing you to connect to the net and find MP3 files.

RealJukebox (http://www.real.com)

This is more of an all-rounder, and costs £29.95 to download. It can play .WAV samples, RealAudio and RealVideo as well as MP3 files, and can also convert tracks on CDs into MP3 or RealAudio files. Again, there is a Custom Playlist function available, which will allow you to catalogue and organise your digital music collection. However, RealJukebox doesn't have the equalisers and other signal-processing effects boasted by Sonique and Winamp.

UnrealPlayer (http://www.303tek.com)

Good sound quality, but it does cost $19.95 to download. Its main selling point is a DJ function that enables the user to create custom outboard effects, such as reverb and delay, although whether this improves the sound is debatable. There is also a graphic equaliser and the standard transport control functions common to all of these players: Play, Pause, Fast Forward, Search and so on.

Windows Media Player (http://www.microsoft.com)

This package is useful for Flash, Shockwave and other streamed audio, while for MP3 files it's a pretty basic no-frills player. If graphic equalisers, custom playlists, skins and add-ons are what you're looking for, then look elsewhere. It's worth downloading for free, though – I use it to listen to live streamed match commentaries from Liverpool FC's web site, but then I don't need a 20-band graphic equaliser to listen to a scouser burbling into a microphone. The Mac version is the QuickTime player, which comes as part of the installation package for all new iMacs and PowerMacs.

MusicMatch Jukebox (http://www.musicmatch.com)

This is one of the most popular players on the market, mainly because of its multi-functional nature, which provides facilities for CD ripping, MP3 encoding and ID3 tag editing as well as the playing of music files. The MP3 encoding and ripping features are its chief selling point – its encoding of MP3 and WMA is faster than its competitors (for instance, a four-minute .WAV file can be encoded into a 128kb MP3 file in less than three minutes).

Because of its cost ($29.95), its not-particularly-well-designed control panel and its absence of signal-processing effects and skins, most users tend to download a freeware player, like Sonique, to play their MP3 files and use MusicMatch Jukebox to do the hard stuff at which it excels – ripping, encoding, building CD compilations and playlists.

computer speakers

Recommended computer speakers:

- Videologic's Sirocco Spirit (http://www.videologic.com);
- Altec Lansing's ADA305 (http://www.alteclansing.com);
- Logitech's Soundman X2 (http://www.logitech.com).

CD writers

The prices of CD writers have dropped over the last couple of years. Manufacturers such as Sony, Philips, Hewlett Packard and Freecom charge around £110-£120 for a basic model, which resembles a car stereo in shape and size. These may be inserted into your PC or connected via the Universal Serial Buss (USB) to your Mac. Alternatively, you could choose to buy the more robust stand-alone model, but you'll be looking to pay around £250.

recommended CD writers

Plextor PXW8220T
Creative Labs CDR4224
Sony CRX120E
Philips CDRW404
TEAC CDR56S
Panasonic CW7501
Yamaha CRW-8424S
Ricoh MP7040A

One of the main decisions to make when purchasing a CD writer is whether to buy a CD-R or CD-RW player.

CD-R and CD-RW

CD-R is short for CD-Recordable. CD-R disks are a form of "write once, read multiple" media that work just like standard CDs. Unlike other types of optical media, CD-Rs can be played in a normal CD player. Whenever you master a record in a post-production studio, you'll be given a CD-R by the engineer to take home and listen to on your stereo so that you can check that you're happy with the mastering process. (Basically, mastering is the first cut of the record, producing a balanced, equalised, edited acetate from which duplicates can be manufactured.) The disadvantage with standard CD-Rs is that you can't reuse the disks – you can only record onto them once.

CD-RW, on the other hand, enables you to erase a disk and reuse it for the recording of different material. However, CD-RW (CD-ReWritable) media won't work in all standard CD players, although CD-RW drives are able to write both CD-R and CD-RW disks. It's thought that CD-RW disks generally give a higher level of reliability than CD-R disks. Whether this is true or not, in practice their main advantage is that, when recording to CD-RW, if the recording fails for any reason you can simply erase the aborted recording and start again.

where to find information about CD writers and burners

http://www.howstuffworks.com
http://www.octave.com/library.html
http://music.digidesign.com/html/faqs/faqmlcd.html
http://www.hrrc.org
http://www.cdpage.com
http://www.westnet.com/~gsmith/cdrecord.htm
http://www.cdarchive.com
http://members.xoom.com/cdburning
http://www.mscience.com
http://www.cdmediaworld.com
http://www.cd-info.com
http://www.osta.org
http://www.adaptec.com/cdrec/
http://www.cdrwcentral.com

where to find CD writers, CD-Rs, hardware and software

http://www.rimage.com
http://www.superduperdisc.com
http://www.compusa.com
http://www.oneoffcd.com
http://www.microtech.com
http://www.uvision.com
http://www.necx.com
http://www.ic-direct.com
http://www.com/mediasource
http://www.cdarchive.com
http://www.cddimensions.com
http://www.commercial-illusions.com
http://www.octave.com
http://www.mediasupply.com
http://www.computability.com
http://www.cd-recordable.com
http://www.cdw.com

key music web sites

where to find MP3 files

http://www.napster.com
http://www.knac.com
http://www.cductive.com
http://www.noisebox.com
http://www.mp3street.com
http://www.peoplesound.com
http://www.musicmaker.com
http://www.vitaminic.com
http://www.emusic.com
http://www.tunes.com
http://www.cdnow.com
http://www.rioport.com
http://www.crunch.co.uk
http://www.mudhut.co.uk
http://www.farmclub.com
http://www.getoutthere.bt.com
http://www.music.lycos.com/mp3
http://www.madasafish.com
http://www.mp3now.com
http://www.listen.com
http://www.jazzpromo.com
http://www.wiredplanet.com
http://www.mp3-uk.com
http://www.audiogalaxy.com
http://www.amp3.com
http://www.takeoutmusic.com
http://www.iuma.com
http://www.gnutella.com
http://www.freenet.com

getting your music heard on the net

http://www.musicunsigned.com
http://www.peoplesound.com
http://www.vitaminic.com
http://www.popwire.com
http://www.mudhut.co.uk
http://www.farmclub.com
http://www.getsigned.com
http://www.bands-online.com
http://www.luma.com
http://www.amp3.com
http://www.bandreg.co.uk
http://www.ubl.com
http://www.getoutthere.bt.com
http://www.artistdirect.com
http://www.hungrybands.com

record labels

A&M
http://www.umusic.com

Acid Jazz Records
http://www.acidjazz.co.uk

Aegean
http://www.aegean.net

Affinity Records
http://www.transatlanticmusic.com

Arista Records
http://www.bmg.com

Astralwerks
http://www.astralwerks.com

Atlantic Records
http://www.atlantic-records.com

Beggars Banquet Records
http://www.beggars.com

Big Chill
http://www.bigchill.co.uk

BMG Entertainment
http://www.bmg.com

Castle Music
http://www.castlemusic.com

Cherry Red Records
http://www.cherryred.co.uk

China Records
http://www.china.co.uk/china

Chrysalis
http://www.emichrysalis.co.uk

City Slang Records
http://www.cityslang.com

Columbia Records
http://www.sonymusic.co.uk

Creation Records
http://www.creation.co.uk

Decca Music Group
http://www.decca.com

Deconstruction
http://www.deconstruction.co.uk

Def Jam
http://www.islanddefjam.com

Distinctive Records
http://www.distinctiverecords.com

Dreamworks
http://www.dreamworks.com

EastWest Records
http://www.eastwest.co.uk

Edel UK Records
http://www.edel.co.uk

Elemental Records
http://www.elemental.music.co.uk

EMI Records
http://www.emichrysalis.co.uk

EMI: Chrysalis
http://www.emichrysalis.co.uk

Epic Records
http://www.sonymusic.co.uk

Epitaph Records
http://www.epitaph.com

Fiction Records
http://www.fictionsongs.com

Finger Lickin' Records
mailto:www.fingerlickin@ukf.net

Flying Rhino Records
http://www.flying-rhino.co.uk

Fontana
http://www.polygram.com

Food Records
http://www.food-records.co.uk

4 Liberty Records
http://www.libertyrecords.co.uk

4AD
http://www.4ad.com

Fundamental Recordings
http://www.fundamental.co.uk

Geffen Records
http://www.umusic.com

Go! Discs
http://www.polygram.com

Grapevine Label
http://www.rmg.com

Higher Ground
http://www.higherground.co.uk

Hollywood Records
http://www.hollywoodrecords.com

Hut Recordings
http://www.raft.vmg.co.uk

Hyperion Records
http://www.hyperion-records.co.uk

Illicit Recordings
http://www.illicitrecordings.com

INCredible
http://www.sonymusic.co.uk

Independiente
http://www.independiente.co.uk

Indochina
http://www.china.co.uk/china

Infectious Records
http://www.infectiousuk.com

Instant Karma
http://www.instantkarma.co.uk

Island Records
http://www.island.co.uk

Interscope
http://www.umusic.com

JBO
http://www.jbo.co.uk

London Records
http://www.londonrecords.co.uk

Mantra
http://www.beggars.com

MCA Records
http://www.umusic.com

Media Records
http://www.nukleuz.com

Mercury Records
http://www.polygram.com

Ministry Of Sound Recordings
http://www.ministryofsound.co.uk

Mo Wax
http://www.mowax.com

Mushroom Records
http://www.mushroomuk.com

Music Collection International
http://www.vci.co.uk

Music For Nations
http://www.music-for-nations.co.uk

Nervous Records
http://www.nervous.co.uk

Ninja Tune
http://www.ninjatune.net

Nukleuz
http://www.nukleuz.com

Nuphonic Records
http://www.nuphonic.co.uk

Nude Records
http://www.nuderecords.com

One Little Indian Records
http://www.indian.co.uk

Parlophone
http://www.parlophone.co.uk

PIAS Recordings
http://www.pias.com

Polydor
http://www.polydor.co.uk

Poptones
http://www.poptones.com

Positiva
http://www.positivarecords.com

Quench Recordings
http://www.subbase.com

RCA
http://www.bmg.com

Receiver Records
http://www.trojan-records.com

Rough Trade Records
http://www.roughtrade.music.co.uk

Rykodisc
http://www.rykodisc.com

Sanctuary Music
http://www.sanctuarygroup.com

Serious Records
http://www.seriousrecords.com

Setanta Records
http://www.setanta.com

Shifty Disco
http://www.shiftydisco.co.uk

Silvertone
http://www.zomba.co.uk

Skint Records
http://www.skint.net

Sony Music Entertainment (UK)
http://www.sonymusic.co.uk

Sony S2
http://www.sonymusic.co.uk

Subversive Records
http://www.subversiverecords.co.uk

Superior Quality
http://www.superiorqualityrecordings.co.uk

Talkin Loud
http://www.polygram.com

Telstar Records
http://www.telstar.co.uk

Tommy Boy
http://www.tommyboy.com

Too Pure
http://www.toopure.com

Tuff Gong
http://www.umusic.com

Triple XXX Recordings
http://www.triplexxx.co.uk

Universal Music International
http://www.umusic.com

Ultimate Dilemma
http://www.ultimate-dilemma.com

Urban Collective
http://www.urbancoll.com

Virgin Records
http://www.vmg.co.uk

V2 Records
http://www.v2music.com

Wall Of Sound Recordings
http://www.wallofsound.net

Warner Music (UK)
http://www.warnermusic.co.uk

Warp Records
http://www.warprecords.com

WEA
http://www.wea.co.uk

Wiiija Records
http://www.wiiija.com

XL Recordings
mailto:www.xl@xl.recordings.com

Zomba Records
http://www.zomba.co.uk

ZTT Records
http://www.ztt.com

radio stations

http://www.bringthenoise.com
http://www.broadcast.com
http://www.xfm.co.uk
http://www.bbc.co.uk/radio1
http://www.virginradio.com
http://www.jazzfm.com
http://www.radioacademy.org
http://www.musicmusicmusic.com
http://www.radio.sonicnet.com
http://www.spinner.com
http://www.virgin.net/radio

http://www.skyjazz.com
http://www.live365.com
http://www.greenwitch.com
http://www.stormlive.com
http://www.music3w.com

music press

NME
http://www.nme.com

Music Week
http://www.dotmusic.com

Q
http://www.q4music.com

Rolling Stone
http://www.rollingstone.com

Billboard
http://www.billboard.com

Metal Hammer
http://www.metalhammer.co.uk

The Wire
http://www.dfuse.com/the-wire

music news

http://www.darkerthanblue.com
http://www.launch.com
http://www.music365.com
http://www.worldpop.com
http://www.onlinepop.co.uk
http://www.musicstation.com/musicnewswire
http://www.bigmouth.co.uk
http://www.electricbasement.com
http://www.mtv.com
http://www.sonicnet.com
http://www.ukmix.net

music retailers

http://www.towereurope.com
http://www.virgin.net
http://www.hmv.co.uk
http://www.getmusic.com
http://www.uk.bol.com
http://www.amazon.com
http://www.cdnow.co.uk
http://www.audiostreet.co.uk
http://www.101cd.com
http://www.indiemusic.co.uk
http://www.cdparadise.com
http://www.darkerthanblue.com
http://www.libertysurf.co.uk
http://www.lineone.net
http://www.megastar.co.uk
http://www.opalmusic.com
http://www.netsounds.com
http://www.screaming.net
http://www.music365.com
http://www.worldonline.co.uk
http://www.onlinerecords.co.uk
http://www.jungle.com
http://www.timeless-music.co.uk
http://www.sisterray.co.uk
http://www.secondspin.com
http://www.action-records.co.uk
http://www.cduniverse.com
http://www.cd999.com
http://www.clickmusic.com
http://www.nextuptech.com

live events and streamed webcasts

http://www.totp.beeb.com
http://www.channelfly.com
http://www.gigsandtours.com
http://www.streamland.co.uk
http://www.ticketweb.co.uk
http://www.liveconcerts.com
http://www.musicvideo.com

http://www.real.com
http://www.sceneone.co.uk
http://www.mtv.co.uk
http://www.gatecrasher.co.uk
http://www.ministryofsound.co.uk
http://www.thebox.co.uk
http://www.vidnet.com
http://www.mediawave.co.uk
http://www.stv.com
http://www.webcasters.org

music organisations

American Society Of Composers, Authors And Publishers (ASCAP)
http://www.ascap.com

Association Of Independent Music (AIM)
http://www.musicindie.com

Association Of Professional Recording Services (APRS)
http://www.aprs.co.uk

British Academy Of Composers And Songwriters (BACAS)
http://www.britishacademy.com

British Phonographic Industry (BPI)
http://www.bpi.co.uk

Broadcast Music Inc (BMI)
http://www.bmi.com

Equity
http://www.equity.org.uk

Incorporated Society Of Musicians (ISM)
http://www.ism.org

International Association Of Entertainment Lawyers (IAEL)
http://www.iael.org

Music Managers Forum (MMF)
http://www.imf-uk.org

Mechanical Copyright Protection Society (MCPS)
http://www.mcps.co.uk

Musicians' Union (MU)
http://www.musiciansunion.org.uk

National Entertainment Agents Council (NEAC)
http://www.neac.urg.uk

Performing Arts Media Rights Association (PAMRA)
http://www.pamra.org.uk

Performing Right Society (PRS)
http://www.prs.co.uk

Phonographic Performance Limited (PPL)
http://www.ppluk.com

Recording Industry Association Of America (RIAA)
http://www.riaa.com

Society Of European Songwriters And Composers (SESAC)
http://www.sesac.com

music databases

http://www.bandreg.co.uk
http://www.ubl.com
http://www.bandnames.com

glossary

AIM

Association of Independent Music. A UK record-industry body formed in 1999, representing a coalition of independent labels and – unlike the major-label equivalent, the PPL – able to offer blanket licences of its members' repertoire to online radio stations.

analogue-digital converter

A device which takes in analogue (electrical) information and converts it into digital (numeric) information, which a computer is then able to understand.

ADSL

Asymmetric Digital Subscriber Line. Allows data transmission on existing copper wires, meaning that information can be transferred at up to ten times pre-ADSL speed.

AOL

America OnLine, America's largest internet service provider. Its proposed merger with Time Warner will make it the world's biggest legitimate internet content provider.

ASCAP

American Society of Composers, Authors and Publishers.

blanket licence

A licence that covers or "blankets" all of the compositions or recordings controlled by an individual licensing organisation, such as the PRS or the MCPS. Obtaining a blanket licence allows you to avoid negotiating on an individual basis with hundreds of different artists, writers and record labels for the right to use their work.

BMI

Broadcast Music Incorporated.

bounty

Another term for a referral fee or commission. The term is used in the context of, for example, a record company paying a bounty to an artist for a record sale from the label's web site which came as a result of the customer following a link from the artist's site.

broadband

Internet connections allowing for the transmission of several channels of data simultaneously at high speeds.

burning

In this context, to transfer data to a CD, for example from an MP3 player in order to archive it. This process involves permanently burning the data onto the CD.

byte

A set of eight digital bits (the smallest items in computer language). Together, they make up the basic digital building block.

CD-R/CD-RW

Compact Disc Recordable and Compact Disc ReWritable. Refers to both the stand-alone player (or a drive built into a PC) and to the individual disks themselves upon which the data is recorded.

codec

Compression/decompression. An algorithm used by MP3 to compress audio data to approximately one twelfth of its normal size and allow it to be decompressed, or restored, on reaching the user's computer.

copyright directive

The endlessly postponed European Union Directive On Copyright And Related Rights In The Information Society, now due to be implemented at some point around the publication of this book. The Directive aims to introduce new rights specifically to cater for the online exploitation of, among other things, music. (See Chapter 11.)

downloading

The digital or electronic delivery of music, or other digital information, via wire or wireless means. This will always result in a copy of the information downloaded being made on the hard drive of the destination computer.

encryption

Encryption technology, such as the use of passwords or watermarking, allows players to recognise and play only legitimate music files, or allows only a limited number of copies to be made (usually one) before the temporary password is withdrawn.

equaliser

An electronic device which increases the contribution of a certain frequency range in a sound, usually displayed graphically (or, occasionally, in wave form) on an MP3 player.

ethernet

A "micro-internet" system, enabling a group of computers in a building to communicate with each other.

filter

An electronic device which decreases the contribution of a certain frequency range in a sound.

fulfilment provider

The e-commerce term for a company responsible for some or all of the following: storing, packing, distributing and the handling of payment.

hypertext linking

A means by which one web page is connected or linked to another, or one web site is connected to another.

IFPI

International Federation of the Phonographic Industry. An anti-piracy body representing the worldwide recording industry, lobbying governments for anti-piracy and copyright protection legislation. (The IFPI has, for example, campaigned vigorously on behalf of rights holders throughout the drafting of the EU Copyright Directive.)

interface

A matching connection. For a computer to connect to another piece of equipment – a printer, for example – a suitable interface must be made. Sometimes known as a port.

ISDN

Integrated Services Digital Network. A very fast alternative digital phone connection, often used in webcasts, although soon to be superseded by ADSL.

ISP

Internet Service Provider. A company that provides access to the internet, such as AOL, Freeserve or AltaVista.

Liquid Audio

A form of compression software, favoured by the record industry over MP3, because it incorporates copyright protection technology. (See "Encryption".)

MCPS

Mechanical Copyright Protection Society.

MIDI

Musical Instrument Digital Interface. A means of controlling one instrument from another, or controlling an instrument from a computer.

MMF

Music Managers Forum.

modem

A modulation/demodulation device that enables computers to communicate via the telephone system.

MP3

Motion Picture Experts Group One Audio Layer Three. A compression/decompression algorithm, or *codec*, used for transmitting audio information via the internet. (See Chapter 2 for a detailed definition of MP3.)

PPD

Published Price to Dealer, more commonly known as dealer price. The method by which royalties are normally calculated on conventional record sales in the UK. The US (and some UK labels) prefer to use the retail price, or SRLP (Suggested Retail List Price), as a basis for calculation. At present, records sold over the internet in physical form and by means of digital download are more likely to result in a royalty based on a percentage of the record label's net receipts. (See Chapter 6.)

PPL

Phonographic Performance Limited. A collective body representing the vast majority of UK record companies, including all of the major labels and many independent labels who are also members of AIM.

PRS

Performing Right Society.

RAM

Random Access Memory. The operating part of a computer's memory, for example the type used in samplers to store sample data. The data will be lost when the power is switched off, because it is volatile. Data which has been loaded into RAM must be stored on a permanent medium, such as a hard drive.

RealAudio

RealNetworks' RealAudio has become the streamed music software player of choice for internet users across the globe.

RIAA

Recording Industry Association of America. The lawsuit-happy US equivalent of the PPL.

Rio

The first mass-market portable MP3 player, manufactured by Diamond Multimedia. Diamond were able to continue producing the Rio after successfully defending a lawsuit brought by the RIAA on behalf of the major US record companies, alleging that the manufacture of a portable MP3 player would encourage copyright infringement.

ripping

The practice of encoding or converting music data on CD into MP3 audio files. Otherwise known as digital extraction.

ROM

Read-Only Memory. Once the contents of ROM have been programmed at the manufacturing stage, they cannot be altered. Unlike RAM, it retains its contents when the power is switched off, because it is non-volatile.

SDMI

Secure Digital Music Initiative. An alliance of record companies and technology providers forged by the RIAA to build and develop a specification for the electronic delivery of music.

skins

Not the rolling variety, but another name for the outer layer or design of the Winamp/Macamp virtual music player. Check out the vast selection at www.winamp.com/skins/index.html.

streaming

The real-time transmission of data to a computer in a manner which doesn't create or store a permanent copy of that data.

unmetered access

Free internet access, a practice common in the States but only gradually taking off in the UK. Alternatively, ISPs offering "flat-rate" access allow you to access the internet for a monthly fee, regardless of the amount of time you spend online or the number of calls you make.

URL

Uniform Resource Locator, the technical term for the address of your web site.

USB

Universal Serial Buss. USB ports are fitted to most modern computers, enabling them to be connected to hardware, such as scanners or CD writers, or to an ADSL connection.

webcast

Webcasting allows you to watch and listen to live (or later) transmissions of live events on your home computer. It's a form of streaming, only with streamed visual information as well as streamed audio.

WMA

Windows Media Audio, Microsoft's own encrypted digital distribution music format.

sources

quotes

Chapter 3: Ian Clarke quote courtesy of *Music Week*.

Chapter 4: Courtney Love quote courtesy of *NME*; Michael Eisner and Kenny Gates quotes courtesy of *Music Week*.

Chapter 5: Sas Metcalfe quote courtesy of *Music Week*; Pete Angelus quote courtesy of *Guitarist Magazine*, August 2000.

Chapter 7: copyright notice courtesy of *Practical Law For Companies*, issue 11(5), 2000. (Article by Clare Shrimpton.)

Chapter 9: Poptones album review by Paul Lester, courtesy of *The Guardian*, 8 September 2000; Matt Jagger quote courtesy of *Music Week*.

Chapter 10: Judge Jed Rakoff quote courtesy of Dotmusic.com.

bibliography

Music Week and Dotmusic.com, 1998-2000
Commercial Law Journal, 1998, issue 8; 1999, issue 3
In-House Lawyer, February 1999; April 2000
Entertainment Law Review, 1998-2000
Electronic Business Law, 1999 issue 1(5); 2000 issue 2(5)
European Intellectual Property Review, issue 22(8), 2000
Legal Studies, issue 19(3), 1999